Lifted

Moments and Mercies that Elevate Us

Lifted

Moments and Mercies that Elevate Us

Susan Chadaz

WALNUT SPRINGS PRESS

But they that wait upon the Lord shall renew their strength;
they shall mount up with wings as eagles; they shall run,
and not be weary; and they shall walk, and not faint.

Isaiah 40:31

Contents

Introduction

As children of God, we came to earth to learn and grow so we can return to live with Him someday. Because we are mortal and subject to opposition, all of us face trials, challenges, and the consequences of sins and mistakes—both ours and those of others. These times can try our faith and might even make us feel like giving up.

The French author Gustave Flaubert wrote, "The principle thing . . . is to keep one's soul aloft" ("To Laure de Maupassant," Paris, 23 Feb. 1873, in *The Letters of Gustave Flaubert*). Just as a kite needs lift in order to soar, we all need lift to rise above the things of the world so that we may see our lives from an eternal perspective.

If we will trust in our perfect, loving Heavenly Father, He will be there to walk through our trials with us. He will send moments that lift us, and He will shower us with tender mercies. These moments and mercies can raise our thoughts to a loftier place from which we can see our possibilities and potential.

There have been days when I have felt down, and days when I have wondered why life can be so hard. But with each of those times has come a moment, a mercy, or an experience that, like wings, lifted me up and set me back on course. In this book I will share some of these things that have lifted me. I hope they will lift you as well.

You Are Enough

The term "enough" refers to a quantity that is sufficient to achieve a purpose. In this competitive world where comparisons are as plentiful as Instagram posts, we might start to think we aren't enough. We might listen to these voices and forget whose we are. The fact is, we were created by the God of the universe, who is our Heavenly Father. He has given each of us gifts, talents, and blessings in an individualized plan to help us achieve the objectives of mortal life. We were born with the God-given ability to achieve the glorious purpose of our existence, which is to qualify, through our faith and through the grace of Jesus Christ, to return to live with Heavenly Father someday.

But maybe you are thinking: "I make mistakes all the time. Yes, I repent of my sins, but I'm not perfect. So . . . am I enough? Will I make it to the celestial kingdom?" Elder J. Devn Cornish of the Seventy answered those questions as follows: "'Yes! You are going to be good enough' and 'Yes, you are going to make it as long as you keep repenting and do not rationalize or rebel.' The God of heaven is not a heartless referee looking for any excuse to throw us out of the game. He is our perfectly loving Father, who yearns more than anything else to have all His children come back home and live with Him as families forever. He truly gave His Only Begotten Son that we might not perish but have everlasting life! (John 3:16.) Please believe, and please take hope and comfort from, this eternal truth. Our Heavenly Father intends for us to make it! That is His work and His glory" ("Am I Good Enough? Will I Make It?", Oct. 2016 General Conference).

Despite the challenge of being blind, a former student of mine believed she was enough. She looked forward to each new day and each new opportunity, focusing on her strengths rather than her shortcomings. Her confidence, patience, and kindness were an inspiration. I was blessed to watch her shine and to see her positive effect on others.

When you need a lift, think about all the things Heavenly Father has given you. Remember how far you have come in your life's journey. If you rely on the Savior and keep trying to improve, you will have what it takes to be victorious. Heavenly Father loves you with an infinite love. You are strong enough to withstand the despair of this world, because you are the Lord's. You are enough.

Beat Defeat

One day I was watching my two grandsons at a wrestling match. They had practiced and felt prepared, but after one grandson lost his first three matches, he really started to doubt himself. As his fourth match started, I prayed he would do better, if only to build his confidence. The first round was good and my grandson fought hard, but his opponent was quicker and stronger. When the referee slapped the mat to declare that the opponent's pin was good, my heart sank. The referee raised the hand of the winner. My grandson hung his head and shook the hand of his opponent, then walked over to shake the hand of the opposing team's coach. Then, with tears in his eyes, my grandson returned to his own coach, who tried to encourage and instruct him.

Soon, two older high school boys stepped onto the mat and began their match. It was obvious these young men had been wrestling for many years. When the whistle blew to end this second match, the loser held his head up and shook his opponent's hand. He had disappointment in his eyes, but it was clear he was a fighter. Smiling, he walked over and shook the hand of the opposing team's coach, congratulating him on the strength of his team. Then the young man headed over to his own coach, who patted him on the back and spoke to him, probably telling him how he could improve for the next match. This young man smiled and nodded as if he was ready to try again. This "loser" wasn't a loser at all—he was a fighter. And in my mind, that made him a winner that day.

As my grandson and I watched the end of this second match, I leaned over to him and said, "Watch the loser." I am sure this wrestler had no idea he was teaching a young man how to keep trying, or that he was encouraging a crowd of onlookers to stay positive even in defeat.

We all have days and experiences that leave us doubting ourselves. Satan is the great instigator of doubt. He urges us to live in self-doubt, uncertainty, distrust, and disbelief, which can lead to hopelessness. But we can choose to "fight the good fight of faith" and "lay hold on eternal life" (1 Timothy 6:12). We can choose, as President James E. Faust said, to look forward to a "future bright with hope" ("This Is Our Day," Apr. 1999 General Conference).

Whenever we take a chance or try to do something we haven't done before, there might be setbacks or challenges along the way. This opposition is an important part of life. But remember to never compare yourself to others. Rather, compare your current self to your past self, so you can measure your progress. You have already overcome a great deal in your life and have learned from defeat. Keep moving forward— you can do it!

Let Him Teach You

In my youth, I had a wonderful Young Women teacher who taught me so much about the gospel of Jesus Christ. One day as I walked home from church after one of this teacher's lessons, I felt a renewed determination to draw closer to Heavenly Father. When I got home, I decided to create a vivid reminder of what He wanted me to do. I got a blank piece of paper and a bright-blue marker and in big letters wrote out the word "PRAY." Then on the bottom, I wrote the question that has guided me throughout my life: "What is Heavenly Father trying to teach me now?" I taped the sign to the headboard of my bed. Every morning and evening, the sign reminded me to pray and to think about what He might want me to learn. Often this led to scripture study and an earnest seeking for understanding.

You will be lifted as you allow yourself to be instructed by the Lord. From the beginning of time, God has taught His children. Deuteronomy 4:36 reads, "Out of heaven he made thee to hear his voice, that he might instruct thee." When we open ourselves to what God wants us to learn, we will be taught from on high. We may be taught directly by the voice of the Spirit as we ponder and pray.

We may be taught by the Spirit as we listen to a talk or lesson at church. During our scripture study, we may learn how to apply a particular verse to what is happening in our life, and maybe another scriptural passage answers a question we have.

There is no limit to the ways God can teach us, but one thing is certain: learning takes diligence and study on our part. We must actually *want* to learn. We must "seek learning, even by study and also by faith" (Doctrine and Covenants 88:118). As we do, we will "find wisdom and great treasures of knowledge, even hidden treasures" (Doctrine and Covenants 89:19).

Put Fear to Flight

Fear can weigh us down and limit our perspective. One year at BYU–Idaho Education Week, I opened my class with the question "What are you afraid of?" I had done a Google search for the top ten things people fear, and I wanted to compare that list with what my Ed Week class attendees would say. It was surprising how different their answers were from the answers in the Google list. The latter included things like heights, dentists, snakes, spiders, flying, enclosed spaces, mice, dogs, thunder and lightning, and public speaking. My students at Education Week mentioned fears such as failure (and success), rejection, debt, isolation, being alone, darkness, sin, and not being with family.

Elder Ronald A. Rasband declared: "Our single adults fear making commitments such as getting married. Young marrieds . . . can fear bringing children into an increasingly wicked world. Missionaries fear lots of things, especially approaching strangers. Widows fear going forward alone. Teenagers fear not being accepted; grade-schoolers fear the first day of school; university students fear getting back a test. We fear failure, rejection, disappointment, and the unknown. We fear hurricanes, earthquakes, and fires that ravage the land and our lives.

We fear not being chosen, and on the flip side, we fear being chosen. We fear not being good enough; we fear that the Lord has no blessings for us" ("Be Not Troubled," Oct. 2018 General Conference).

If we let fear guide our lives, we will become familiar with fear's friends—discouragement, anger, disappointment, despair, doubt, and failure. Dwelling on these negative emotions eventually causes us to lose confidence in Heavenly Father's love for us.

The only way to dispel fear is to exercise faith in God. You can do this by obeying him and by following the counsel of His living prophets. It is my testimony that God lives, that He loves you, and that His work and His glory are to "bring to pass [*your*] immortality and eternal life" (Moses 1:39).

The third verse of "How Firm a Foundation" (*Hymns*, no. 85) reads:

Fear not, I am with thee; oh, be not dismayed
For I am thy God and will still give thee aid.
I'll strengthen thee, help thee and cause thee to stand,
Upheld by my righteous, upheld by my righteous,
Upheld by my righteous, omnipotent hand.

Fear is put to flight as we look to God in everything. As the Lord Himself counseled, "Look unto me in every thought; doubt not, fear not" (Doctrine and Covenants 6:36).

Prepare Him Room

A favorite Christmas hymn helped me learn more about how I can live closer to Christ.

Joy to the world, the Lord is come;
Let earth receive her King!
Let ev'ry heart prepare him room.
("Joy to the World" [*Hymns*, no. 201])

As I read that verse, I stopped at "Let ev'ry heart prepare him room," and read it again. I thought about the words and wondered if I was leaving room in my life to receive Christ. Like you, I have a busy life with my job, Church callings, family responsibilities, and many other things. But reading this verse of "Joy to the World" prompted me to make more room for Christ by studying the scriptures more often.

I have read the scriptures since I was young, and I vividly remember underlining verses with my first red pencil. I made a bag to carry my scriptures in when I walked home from Primary and, later, Young Women classes. After I got married, my husband and I regularly read the scriptures together. When we had children, and as they grew up, we would ring the triangle hanging on the coat rack to signal that it was time for family scripture study.

But in all of my scripture reading, I don't think I ever truly feasted on the word until recently. Now I am preparing room for Jesus Christ in my life by taking the time to really *study* the scriptures. President Russell M. Nelson has asked us to make an adjustment in our lives, our schedules, our days—to prepare room for the Lord. President Nelson declared, "As Latter-day Saints, we have become accustomed to thinking of 'church' as something that happens in our meetinghouses, supported by what happens at home. We need an adjustment to this pattern" ("Opening Remarks," Oct. 2018 General Conference).

Once I began regularly feasting upon the scriptures instead of occasionally snacking on them, I discovered the strength and power of the word of God. Now I read the scriptures every day—and I look forward to it very much.

I challenge you to make time to study the scriptures every day, if you're not already doing this. Set a specific time of day, and don't let anything interfere with this sacred goal. As you prepare room for the Lord by feasting upon His words, you will feel an increase of the Spirit in your life.

Make the World Better

Years ago, someone knocked on our door and wanted to speak to my husband, Steve. Our son had answered the door, and because I was in another room, I didn't see the visitor. Steve's conversation with the person lasted only a few minutes, and after I heard the door close, I asked my husband who the visitor was. He explained that the woman lived in another state and was passing through town. Her family had stopped at the local McDonald's, and she had checked the phone book to see if Steve Chadaz still lived in Tremonton. She told my husband that she had been a classmate of his at Bear River High School and had wanted to thank him for being kind to her. She said there had been many days at school when she had felt alone and unnoticed, but then Steve would smile at her and say hi. She had stopped by our home twenty years later to thank him and tell him what a difference his kindness had made in her life. Though he remembered her from school, Steve had no memory of going out of his way to show her extra kindness. It was wonderful to learn of the difference he had made in someone's life without even knowing it. He hadn't done anything big or extravagant; he had simply smiled and said hello.

President David O. McKay stated: "Throughout the world, men, women, and children spend their lives searching to attain one common goal. We hunt for it, seek it, rummage around and pursue it and sometimes we even find it only to discover the prize as short-lived, transitory and passing. All mankind desires happiness. And in the chase for happiness, there is one simple secret that will direct our search. Specifically stated, this law is, 'We live our lives most completely when we strive to make the world better and happier' for another" (*Teachings of Presidents of the Church: David O. McKay*, Chapter 19, "The Divine Nature of Service," 2003, 2011).

A favorite hymn of mine is "A Poor Wayfaring Man of Grief" (*Hymns*, no. 29). The summer after I graduated from high school, a few of my friends and I found summer jobs at the cherry cannery in Perry, Utah. It was my first opportunity to work on an assembly line, and that summer I learned much about patience and persistence. One of our assignments was to make sure all of the cherries, which came down through funnels, dropped into the cans. Needless to say, this was a very tedious task. After a few hours of watching cherries drop, my friends and I wondered how we could pass the time. One worker suggested that we memorize all seven verses of "A Poor Wayfaring Man of Grief." To this day I still remember all the words. The message of this beautiful hymn has helped me strive to serve others throughout my life.

A poor, wayfaring Man of grief
Hath often crossed me on my way,
Who sued so humbly for relief
That I could never answer nay.
I had not pow'r to ask his name,

Whereto he went, or whence he came;
Yet there was something in his eye
That won my love; I knew not why.

In the Book of Mormon, King Benjamin taught, "Behold, I tell you these things that ye may learn wisdom; that ye may learn that when ye are in the service of your fellow beings ye are only in the service of your God" (Mosiah 2:2).

"Today while the sun shines," look for opportunities to serve others, to "[c]heer and bless and brighten, every passing day" ("Scatter Sunshine," *Hymns,* no. 230). Visit a neighbor who needs a friend. Help a stranger who crosses your path. Be kind to those with whom you live, work, and worship. These acts can change both the giver and the receiver for good.

The Grace of God

While walking to class one winter day when I was in college, I came across a car stuck in the snow. Several students had already stopped to help. With their backpacks set aside, they tried to push the vehicle out of the snow, but after numerous attempts, they still couldn't budge the car. As these Good Samaritans prepared to try again, one young man took a "superhero" stance—feet firmly planted, a fisted left hand at his side, and his right hand raised. Then in a loud voice, he shouted, "We have the power to move this beast!" And they did.

As members of the Lord's Church in the last dispensation of the gospel, we have great responsibilities. To meet these responsibilities, we often need power beyond our own mortal abilities and strength. This power is the grace of God. It is the power by which we overcame Satan, the great dragon, in the pre-existence. "And there was war in heaven: Michael and his angels fought against the dragon; and the dragon fought and his angels and prevailed not . . . and the great dragon was cast out . . . And they overcame him by the blood of the Lamb, and by the word of their testimony" (Revelation 12:7–11). We can have that same strength today.

Scholar Carol Cornwall Madsen said: "How often has God told us, *My grace is sufficient for you?* (See Ether 12:27.) Do we ever really ponder what that means? I think he wants us to give grace its due in our lives, to yield ourselves to that unearned blessing more often so that it might lighten our spiritual load and diminish our sense of inadequacy. I think it means to depend more than we do on the enabling power of God's grace to accept and meet our daily commitments" ("In the Covenant of Grace," BYU Women's Conference, 1993).

When you feel down, ask your Heavenly Father for the power to continue forward in faith. This power—this grace—is available because of the great atoning sacrifice of Jesus Christ. His grace can "set [your] feet upon a rock" (Psalm 40:2) and give you the strength to meet your daily responsibilities and to further God's work on the earth.

Lift and Be Lifted

Several years ago, I was asked to participate in our stake's pioneer trek for youth. After many months of preparation, the first day of the trek finally arrived. Dressed in our pioneer clothes, we packed the handcarts, and soon the journey began. We talked, laughed, and sang as we pushed and pulled our handcarts. However, as the hours grew on, the voices quieted and the singing stopped. The July weather was hot, and we ended up having to walk more miles the first day than planned. Despite this, the youth were amazing and did not quit. The leaders kept encouraging us and told us that we would soon be at base camp, which was always "just beyond the next hill." Many "next hills" later, the steepest incline of the day lay before us. I wondered how we could ever push our handcarts up the hill, with so much of our strength already spent.

Then one of the leaders announced that this was the "women's pull." Priesthood leaders and young men were asked to step aside and not give any assistance while the women pulled the handcarts up the hill on their own. The men and boys quietly moved away from the handcarts, and with worry and concern on their faces, they walked alongside the girls and women. Some of the young men hurried to the top of the hill so they could take the handcarts back from the women as soon as they crested the peak of the hill.

It was amazing to witness the grit, determination, and fortitude of these youth. After my handcart was safely to the top, I stopped and rested at the side of the road. However, the priesthood and young men did not rest. As each handcart crested the hill, the young men immediately took over and pulled the handcart across the ridge. Going back again and again, they worked tirelessly, pushing and pulling each handcart.

Watching with admiration and reverence, I wondered what I could do to help. Then I remembered an orange I had saved from lunch. I removed it from my pocket, peeled it, and passed out one section at a time to the weary young men on the "rescue teams." One by one, each of these modern-day pioneers thanked me for the treat. How I wished I had more to give! With one last section of orange in my hand, I approached the next young man coming along the trail. A cowboy hat hid his face as he pushed his handcart. Suddenly he stopped, lifted his head, and said, "Thanks, Mom." The boy was my own son. With tears in my eyes, I put the orange slice in his mouth, gave him a quick hug, and watched as he continued on. I will always treasure this tender moment. In Matthew 25:50, the Lord declared, "Inasmuch as ye have done it unto one of the least of these my brethren, ye have done it unto me." As I attempted to serve others that day on the pioneer trek, the Lord blessed me with the opportunity to serve one of my own children.

When we love and lift the people around us, we can't help but be lifted ourselves. In the process, we become more like Jesus Christ. Everything He did during His mortal ministry was for people other than Himself. Trying our best to emulate His selflessness will bring us joy beyond measure.

Forgive Anyway

One night after the kids were in bed, my husband and I had a disagreement. I don't remember what it was about, but feelings were hurt and tears were shed, and there didn't seem to be a solution. Before long, I walked into the living room and sat on the couch to think.

The hour was late and the house was quiet. After a while, I knelt and asked my Father in Heaven for guidance and help. Then I took a deep breath and sat silently with my eyes closed. Soon an answer came, and it wasn't at all what I had expected. The Spirit simply said to forgive. And then I was told to go tell my husband how much I loved him. I sat there with tears in my eyes, then I nodded my head and stood up. Immediately the heavy feeling in my heart began to dissipate. With every step I took, my spirit grew lighter—all because of the power of forgiveness.

It is not easy to forgive. When we are offended, the natural man or woman in us tends to go into "fight or flight" mode, which usually means we fight back or run away, and then we hold a grudge. When someone has upset us, hurt our feelings, or insulted us, we can become bitter and angry. These feelings can negatively affect every aspect of our life. Holding back forgiveness can consume us and make us miserable—even though we are not the one who committed the initial sin or offense. If we allow these feelings to persist, we lose the companionship of the Spirit of God.

President Thomas S. Monson declared: "The spirit must be freed from tethers so strong and feelings never put to rest, so that the lift of life may give buoyancy to the soul. In many families, there are hurt feelings and a reluctance to forgive. It doesn't really matter what the issue was. It cannot and should not be left in injure. Blame keeps wounds open. Only forgiveness heals" ("Hidden Wedges" Apr. 2002 General Conference).

When we let go of the "tethers" that pull us down—grudges, resentment, and blame, we will have what President Monson calls "the lift of life" that will give "buoyancy to the soul" (ibid). I love the word *buoyancy*, which refers to the power to keep something afloat, an upward pressure, lightness or resilience of the spirit, and cheerfulness (see Dictionary.com).

If we repent, Heavenly Father forgives our sins. But as part of showing Him that we are truly repentant, we are required to forgive others (see Doctrine and Covenants 64:10). By forgiving those who have trespassed against us, we allow them the same privilege we seek of Heavenly Father—the privilege of being forgiven. Both repentance and forgiveness are essential to our eternal salvation.

Elder Henry B. Eyring said: "It is not true that the behavior of others removes our responsibility for our own. God's standards for our behavior are unchanged whether or not others choose to rise to them. That becomes especially difficult when others hurt us, and we feel justified in our anger. It is a lie that our anger justifies our impulse to hurt or ignore our antagonists. We are to forgive to be forgiven. To wait for them to repent before we forgive and repent is to allow them to choose for us a delay which could cost us happiness here and hereafter" ("Do Not Delay," October 1999 General Conference).

Try the word of God today and allow your spirit to be buoyed up through the power of forgiveness. If someone has hurt you, put aside your bitterness and forgive that person. The heaviness in your heart will depart and your soul will feel the "lift of life" that will "give buoyancy to your soul" (Monson, ibid).

Take Heart

Shadows lengthen in the stadium as the track meet draws to a close. The winners of the final race have crossed the finish line, and the last runners are getting close. Several coaches, teammates, and parents remain, watching and waiting. Imagine a race where the last runners are nearing the finish line, and the crowd stands up to yell, "Quit! You can't do it! Give up! There is no need to push yourself now." The runners begin to sag. Their spirits droop, their heads hang down, and they slowly walk off the track.

No track meet happens like that. Instead, the runners enter their last lap with coaches, teammates, and parents cheering them on and encouraging them to finish the race. "Go on! Only a little way to go! You can do it! You're almost there. Don't give up. Keep going! We believe in you!"

Despite the runners' exhaustion, and regardless of their position, they take heart at the words of encouragement. These competitors' pace quickens as they move forward with a new resolve that only runners understand. Then my favorite part of the race happens—the sprint to the finish. The Apostle Paul taught, "Know ye not that they which run in a race run all, but one receiveth the prize? Run, that ye may obtain" (1 Corinthians 9:24).

I love track meets and am always fascinated at the drive and willpower of the runners—especially at the end of a long race. Just when fatigue and discouragement seem to have the upper hand, the runners' determination somehow intensifies and increases. Stamina and staying power push back weakness, and in that moment, runners become something more than they thought they could be. And they sprint to the finish.

When you feel tired or overwhelmed, when Satan tells you to quit—that you can't do it and should give up—think about the runners on a track and their determination to finish the race. One of the most inspirational verses in the Old Testament explains that "the race is not to the swift, nor the battle to the strong" (Ecclesiastics 9:11). The Lord and His prophets teach us that those who endure to the end shall be saved. The race of life is not a sprint, nor is it even a middle-distance run. It is a marathon. So on those days when your legs are tired, your heart is weary, and you feel like walking off the track, hold on and stay on course. Your Father in Heaven is there, cheering you forward: "You can do it. You're almost there. Don't give up. I love you. I believe in you. You are my child."

Watching over Me

On a wall in my house, I painted a large family tree, complete with leaves and branches. Framed photographs of my family—parents, grandparents, sisters, brothers, and generations of ancestors—are attached to the wall so as to appear as if they are hanging from the tree's branches. One day as I was working on my computer, the screen reflected the faces in the portraits on the wall behind me. It seemed as if my family members were looking over my shoulder to see what I was doing. It felt as if they were lovingly watching over me.

Elder Henry B. Eyring stated that "many [people] have discovered that giving of their time to do family history research and temple work has deepened their testimony of the plan of salvation. It has increased the influence of the Spirit in their lives and decreased the influence of the adversary. It has helped them feel closer to their families and closer to the Lord Jesus Christ. They have learned that this work saves not just the dead; it saves all of us (see Doctrine and Covenants 128:18)" ("Gathering the Family of God," Apr. 2017 General Conference).

Each time I do family history work, I learn more about my ancestors—who they really were. Their stories and their lives seem to surround me, so I don't feel alone. I am so grateful for my family—for the generations linked together forever, family to family.

Learn more about your grandparents, your great-grandparents, and other generations that have gone on before. As you do so, and as you find any ancestors who are missing from your family tree, you will grow to love and appreciate them as real people who lived real lives.

Your ancestors are watching over you. As Elder Eyring said on another occasion, "Their hearts are bound to you; their hope is in your hands" ("Hearts Bound Together," Apr. 2005 General Conference).

Entrusted with Truth

Right after my oldest son and his wife were married, they moved to Laie, Hawaii, to attend BYU–Hawaii. The next year, my husband and I flew over to see them and to meet our first grandchild. On Sunday, we attended sacrament meeting with them at their young married students ward. For the musical number that day, the bishop invited all the fathers to come to the front of the chapel and sing a song. Our son was holding his new baby, so instead of waking him up, he simply carried him to the front of the room. Many other fathers holding their own sleeping babies did the same thing. The prelude for the song began, and I knew this would be an unforgettable moment. The song these fathers sang that day was "We'll Bring the World His Truth" (*Children's Songbook*, no. 172).

We have been born, as Nephi of old,
To goodly parents who love the Lord.
We have been taught, and we understand,
That we must do as the Lord commands
We are as the army of Helaman.

We have been taught in our youth.
And we will be the Lord's missionaries
To bring the world his truth.

That day in Hawaii with tears in my eyes, I thought of a time years before when my son was young and sang this same song in Primary. But as I witnessed this older army of Helaman, this army of young fathers, the Spirit bore witness to me that they did understand the Lord's commands, and that now as fathers themselves, entrusted with the truth, they would pass on the teachings of Jesus Christ to their own children.

Helaman described his army as follows (and I don't think there is a more favorable description of anyone in the scriptures, except for the Lord Himself): "They were exceedingly valiant for courage, and also for strength and activity; but behold, this was not all—they were men who were true at all times in whatsoever thing they were entrusted. Yea, they were men of truth and soberness, for they had been taught to keep the commandments of God and to walk uprightly before him" (Alma 53:20–21).

Likewise you, as a valiant member of the Lord's Church, can continue in "whatsoever thing you are entrusted," to learn truth, to live truth, and to pass on truth to the next generation. There is no doubt in my mind that the "youth of the noble birthright," and many Saints who are no longer in their youth, will indeed "carry on, carry on, carry on!" (*Hymns*, no. 255).

Healing in His Wings

When my children were young and one of them would fall and scrape a knee or a hand, he or she would come running to me. Most of the time, once I had wiped away tears, offered soothing words and a kiss, and applied a bandage if needed, the "owie" was all better, and the child would soon be off playing again. Other times, the child's injuries needed more than what I could give—a broken arm from falling off a slippery slide, a badly cut knee from a bike crash, and so on. Of course, there are some injuries we can't see—broken hearts, bruised feelings, and shattered dreams. Those are another category entirely.

In the New Testament, we learn of a woman who had suffered for twelve years from an issue of blood. She had spent all of her money searching for a cure, but to no avail. When she heard that Jesus of Nazareth was near, it must have been her strong faith and perhaps her last ounce of hope that pushed her through a large crowd of people to reach Him. For the rest of the story, we go to Luke's account: "And Jesus said, Who touched me? . . . Somebody hath touched me: for I perceive that virtue is gone out of me. And when the woman saw that she was not hid, she came trembling, and falling down before him, she declared unto him before all the people for what cause she had touched him, and how she was healed immediately. And he said unto her, Daughter, be of good comfort: thy faith hath made thee whole; go in peace" (Luke 8:45, 48).

As a small child reaches out to a parent for healing, this woman reached out to the Savior of the world. Speaking of this miraculous healing, Elder Dennis B. Neuenschwander said: "Though buried among the thronging mass, [the woman] resolutely and quietly pressed forward with a single purpose in mind: to come to the Savior, having faith that He had the power to heal her, that He cared about her and would respond to her need. In this one thing she set herself apart from the crowd. The crowd came to see, but the woman came to be healed" ("One Among the Crowd," Apr. 2008 General Conference).

Sometimes healing comes quickly, and sometimes it takes time. But whatever it is we are going through, we can turn to Jesus Christ, who understands everything we suffer because He suffered it first: "And he shall go forth, suffering pains and afflictions and temptations of every kind; and this that the word might be fulfilled which saith he will take upon him the pains and the sicknesses of his people. And he will take upon him death, that he may loose the bands of death which bind his people; and he will take upon him their infirmities, that his bowels may be filled with mercy, according to the flesh, that he may know according to the flesh how to succor his people according to their infirmities" (Alma 7:11–12).

With healing in His wings (see 2 Nephi 25:13), the Savior truly knows how to succor you. He will give you the strength to endure and to carry on. Reach out to Heavenly Father and ask Him to manifest the Savior's healing and enabling power in your life.

Love Matters Most

Whom do you love? I love Heavenly Father and Jesus Christ with all my heart. I love my family—those I get to see now, those I will get to see again someday, and those still to come. I love grandsons and granddaughters who are growing up too fast. I love babies with little toes and two-year olds with attitudes. I love my friends and my ward members and the people in my neighborhood. I love students who try . . . and students who try me.

Of everything that matters in this life, love matters most—love for God, for our neighbors, for ourselves. The Savior declared: "Thou shalt love the Lord thy God with all thy heart, and with all thy soul, and with all thy mind. This is the first and great commandment. And the second is like unto it, thou shalt love thy neighbor as thyself" (Matthew 22:37–39).

It is not always easy to love everyone. There are days when you might feel "smitten, or despitefully used" (Luke 6:27–29). One night during the holidays, our home teacher (now he would be called our ministering brother) stopped by. During his visit, he mentioned that all his outside Christmas lights had been stolen from his yard. My children were young and asked many questions about the incident. This kind man answered their questions with a lesson about love that my children will never forget. Instead of being angry, this brother said he wished the person who took the lights would have knocked on his door, because he would have given them the lights and more if they needed it.

Let us remember the first and second great commandments. Jesus Christ exemplified this kind of love. He suffered and died for us because of His love for us and for His Father. President Dieter F. Uchtdorf said: "Because love is the great commandment, it ought to be at the center of all and everything we do in our own family, in our Church callings, and in our livelihood. Love is the healing balm that repairs rifts in personal and family relationships. It is the bond that unites families, communities, and nations. Love is the power that initiates friendship, tolerance, civility, and respect. It is the source that overcomes divisiveness and hate. Love is the fire that warms our lives with unparalleled joy and divine hope. Love should be our walk and our talk" ("The Love of God," Oct. 2009 General Conference).

In all of our daily tasks and responsibilities, let us remember that love matters most. When we show love as we speak and interact with others, we and they are lifted. When we show love for our Heavenly Father and His Son Jesus Christ, we can feel a joy that is indescribable. Just as we need to nourish our bodies with food every day, our spirits need the daily nourishment of love. "For this is the message that ye heard from the beginning, that we should love one another (1 John 3:11).

Kites and Counting Blessings

One year at school, I had been teaching my students about setting goals. I wanted to encourage them to set a goal to reach higher in math and reading, so I came up with an idea and gave each student a kite. The children were excited, especially those who had never flown a kite. We discussed the basics of kite flying, then put the kites together. Next, we talked at length about the importance of not letting the strings of one kite get tangled with the strings of another kite. We headed outside with high hopes. The sky was blue, and a light breeze was blowing. However, it didn't take long before the kite-flying lesson became a chaotic scene of tangled kite strings, torn kites, and tears on the faces of children.

Soon, we went back into the classroom to untangle and repair the kites. After I reminded the students not to stand so close to each other while flying their kites, we headed outside to try again. The wind had picked up a little, and all of the children managed to fly their kites. It was amazing to see not only all the kites in the air, but the smile on each child's face.

Like flying kites, life is not always easy. Things don't always just go up and stay up. Sometimes we have to start over and try again. One thing I try to do is to look for God's blessings every day. Blessings are evidence of His love for His children. As we obey Him, and sometimes through no effort on our own, He confers divine favor upon us and pours down blessings from heaven. When we notice and appreciate His blessings, we can't help but know that He loves us.

A wonderful scripture from the Old Testament seems to apply here, with a few words added: "Behold, I go forward, but [sometimes] he is not there. I go backward, but [sometimes] I cannot perceive him. But he knoweth the way that I take: When he that tried me, tested me, proved me. . . . I shall come forth as gold. For my foot hath held his steps. His way have I kept. His way I have not declined. I have esteemed the words of his mouth. For he performeth the thing that is appointed for me" (Job 23:9–14).

In every frustration, in every tangle, and in every tear you shed as you go through the lessons of mortality, God is always with you. Whatever your trial or problem, His grace can heal and restore you, for you "can do all things through Christ which strengtheneth [you])" (Philippians 4:13).

In the Hand of God

After driving all day, my husband Steve and I arrived in Nauvoo, Illinois, where we were scheduled to help our son and his family move back East for school. Steve and I were exhausted and anxious to check into our hotel for the night but couldn't resist driving through old Nauvoo. The beautiful Nauvoo temple came into view, and we were excited to see the rest of the historic city the next day. We were about to turn the car around and head to the hotel when a man in an orange vest waved us forward. Since he looked official, we followed his instructions. Then another orange-vested man motioned for us to turn right. The same thing happened again and then again, and around every corner we watched for the road construction we assumed was going on. Before long, we had joined a long line of cars being directed into an empty field to park.

Obviously, this wasn't road work. My husband parked the car as directed and we got out of the vehicle to ask the people next to us what was going on. After we told them our story, they smiled and said that we were just in time for the Nauvoo Pageant. Until that moment, Steve and I had no idea there was a pageant that night. But since we were already there, we grabbed our jackets and joined the crowd.

The pageant was wonderful, in the midst of Nauvoo and with the temple as the backdrop. The Spirit was so strong as the actors who portrayed Joseph and Hyrum Smith walked down the steps of the stage and through the center of the audience, right next to where my husband and I sat. When we finally made it back to our hotel that night, we talked about how grateful we were to have a chance to see the pageant, and how we had literally been directed to it by the men in orange vests.

Just as Steve and I were led that night, all of God's children can be led by His Son Jesus Christ, who is the Good Shepherd. In 1 Nephi 22:25 we read, "And he gathereth his children from the four quarters of the earth; and he numbereth his sheep, and they know him; and there shall be one fold and one shepherd; and he shall feed his sheep, and in them they shall find pasture."

In order to follow the Savior, we must recognize and listen for His voice. We must place our hand in the hand of God. And as we allow Him to lead us, let us have the courage to accept His will. The poet Minnie Louise Haskins wrote:

And I said to the man who stood at the gate of the year: "Give me a light that I may tread safely into the unknown."
And he replied, "Go out into the darkness and put your hand into the Hand of God.
That shall be to you better than light and safer than a known way."

*So, I went forth, and finding the Hand of God, trod gladly into
    the night.
And He led me toward the hills and the breaking of day in the
    lone East.*

("The Gate of the Year," in James Dalton Morrison, ed.,
    Masterpieces of Religious Verse [New York City:
    HarperCollins, 1948], 92)

Stand in Holy Places

I love to see the temple glowing on a dark night. I love to walk around the beautiful grounds of the temple. But most of all I love the opportunity to enter the house of the Lord and spend time there. The temple allows me to feel the Spirit of the Lord on days when I need to know I am not alone. I love the smiles on the faces of the people who serve in the temple. These brothers and sisters are like angels on earth, kindly and reverently serving God's children on both sides of the veil.

Years ago, my family and I visited Palmyra, New York, and went to the Hill Cumorah Visitors' Center. Two young missionaries gave a short lesson on the purpose of temples. They asked, "Why does The Church of Jesus Christ of Latter-day Saints build temples?" Then they answered their own question with a scripture. I didn't have anything to write down the scripture reference but was determined to remember it, so I repeated the first part of the verse over and over again in my mind until I got home.

Why *do* we have temples? The scripture verse the missionaries read that day gives the answer: "And the great God has had mercy on us, and, made these things known unto us that we might not perish; yea, and he has made these things known unto us beforehand, because he loveth our souls as well as he loveth our children; therefore, in his mercy he doth visit us by his angels, that the plan of salvation might be made known unto us as well as unto future generations" (Alma 24:14).

While Wilford Woodruff was serving a mission, he learned that the Kirtland Temple had been dedicated. He wrote in his journal that this news was "glorious in the first degree" ("An Epistle to the Members of The Church of Jesus Christ of Latter-day Saints," *Millennial Star*, 14 Nov., 1887, 730–31). Later Elder Woodruff exclaimed, "No right feeling Latter-day Saint can think upon this subject without being thrilled with heavenly joy for what God has done for us in our generation, furnishing us, as He has done, with every facility to prepare us, our posterity and our ancestors for that eternal world which lies beyond the present life . . . praise to God should ascend from every heart" (ibid).

Because of His great love for us, our Father in Heaven has provided the sealing power of the priesthood so that families can be sealed together forever in His holy temples. This is a grand and important key in God's great plan of happiness. As we live our lives "Looking for that blessed hope, and the glorious appearing of the great God and our Savior Jesus Christ" (Titus 2:13), we will be lifted by the covenants we have made in holy temples. As Russell M. Nelson has said, "Obedience to the sacred covenants made in temples qualifies us for eternal life—the greatest gift of God to man" ("Prepare for Blessings of the Temple," *Ensign*, Mar. 2002).

If you are feeling down, look toward the temple. If you haven't been inside the temple for a while, get ready and go. Then let the temple lift you.

U-Turns Allowed

Like most people, I've had to make my share of U-turns. In fact, when someone asks me "How did your trip go?", my reply is often something like "I only had to make six U-turns, so it went great."

After driving our oldest son out East for medical school, my husband Steve and I were on our way back to Utah. In Ohio, road construction forced us to leave the freeway and drive through a small town. It was July, and American flags were flying on the porches of many of the old Victorian homes. Steve pulled over because it was my turn to drive, and soon after we traded places, we were back on the freeway. Steve quickly fell asleep. Two hours later I realized that the shadows of the trees were on the wrong side of the vehicle if I was driving west. I woke up Steve, who glanced out the window, and then at me, and then at his watch. It turned out I had been driving in the wrong direction for two hours. I made a U-turn and we began heading in the right direction.

There will be days when you will find yourself lost—physically or emotionally or spiritually. Maybe you have drifted off course or feel abandoned or left behind. When we go through tough times, the adversary wants us to think that *all* is lost. Figuratively speaking, he would have us think there is a sign stating, No U-turns Allowed. And indeed, we read in Mosiah 16:14, that because of sin, "all mankind were lost; and . . . would have been endlessly lost were it not that God redeemed his people from their lost and fallen state." But in His great mercy, Heavenly Father sent His Son Jesus Christ to "redeem his people from their lost and fallen state" (Mosiah 16:4). Thanks to the Savior's glorious Atonement, each of us can make course corrections in our lives, as many times as we need to. In fact, not only is this allowed, but turning away from sin and changing course—repenting—is something Heavenly Father commands us to do.

As you go through life with its challenges and temptations, there will always be a way to turn around and begin again when you make a mistake or take the wrong path. In fact, changing and becoming better is the very purpose of your life on earth. Yes, U-turns are definitely allowed here.

Finding Families

When I was a little girl, I wanted to grow up to be a detective. Each day as my friend Roxanne and I walked home from school, we passed an old, scary house that we thought was haunted. We knew nothing about the people who lived there, but we imagined they were scary too. One day, with friends looking on, Roxanne and I bravely crept up the stairs of the old house and knocked on the door. We quickly lost our nerve and would have run away, but suddenly the doorknob turned. Our feet froze, and we looked up as the door creaked open. Smiling down at Roxanne and me was a beautiful, silver-haired lady. "Hello there," she said. "Can I help you?"

While Roxanne asked the lady if she had seen a lost cat, I peeked into the living room. The walls were painted pink, and there was a fresh vase of flowers on the kitchen table. Sitting at the table was a silver-haired gentleman, and he smiled and waved at me. I found myself waving back. The lady said she would be happy to keep her eye out for our lost cat, and after saying goodbye, Roxanne and I left, humbled to the core.

Walking home that day, I thought about how the haunted house wasn't haunted at all. I wondered about the sweet elderly couple who lived there. They were nice, normal people, and my aspirations to be a professional detective were forever crushed.

Later on, I developed an interest in solving another kind of mystery. For most of my adult life I have tried to bring families together through family history research. My heart has been turned—as have my head, my feet, and my energy—to doing this work.

There is a verse from the Old Testament that is repeated in the New Testament, the Book of Mormon, the Doctrine and Covenants, and Joseph Smith—History. This verse is Malachi 4:6: "And he shall turn the heart of the fathers to the children, and the heart of the children to their fathers, lest I come and smite the earth with a curse."

President Boyd K. Packer taught about the great importance of this work when he said: "Family history work in one sense would justify itself even if one were not successful in clearing names for temple work. The process of searching, the means of going after those names, would be worth all the effort you could invest" ("Your Family History: Getting Started," *Ensign*, Aug. 2003, 17).

Regularly set aside a few hours in your busy life to learn about your ancestors. Find out everything you can about their lives. You will feel a special connection to these people and will find yourself wanting to serve them. But watch out—family history can be addicting!

The Friends He Sends

I love live theater. One year I bought two season tickets to a local theater and planned to take someone with me to each performance. The date for one show drew near, and I still hadn't managed to find someone who could go. My daughter, aunt, and sister were all busy with other things. I was nervous to go alone and wondered if I should just stay home and forfeit both tickets, but in the end I decided to go. I picked up my ticket at Will Call, and the usher directed me to my seat. It was almost curtain time, so I sat down quietly, hoping not to disturb any of the other patrons. Just then, a voice next to me said, "Well, we're glad you finally made it." In surprise, I turned to the person sitting next to me, expecting to see a familiar face, but instead I saw the kind smile of a sweet older lady I had never met. At my perplexed expression, she introduced herself and her daughter, who was sitting next to her. I smiled and said I was happy to meet them. Then the theater lights dimmed, and I settled in to watch the show.

At intermission, my new friend and I started talking. She said her husband had passed away, and then she asked why the chair next to me was empty. I told her a little about myself, and we continued chatting like old friends.

After the show, this lovely lady invited me to go out to dinner with her and her daughter. I was so impressed with their kindness and friendship to a total stranger. I believe that Heavenly Father placed these women in the seats next to me so I wouldn't be alone.

One of my favorite quotes is from President Spencer W. Kimball. He taught: "God does notice us, and he watches over us. But it is usually through another mortal that he meets our needs. Therefore, it is vital that we serve each other" (*The Teachings of Spencer W. Kimball,* ed. Edward L. Kimball [Salt Lake City: Deseret Book Co., 1982], 252).

Keep an eye out for friends the Lord sends to lift you, and watch for opportunities and promptings to be a friend to someone in need.

Sing Your Way Home

In Robert Fulghum's best-selling book *All I Really Need to Know, I Learned in Kindergarten* (New York City: Villard Books, 1988), some of the topics include "Play Fair, Don't Hit," "Warm Cookies and Cold Milk Are Good for You," "Hold Hands," and "Stick Together."

If I were to write a book like Fulghum's, it would be titled *All I Really Need to Know, I Learned in Singing Time.* I enjoyed Primary and loved the songs we sang. As I walked home from school, kicking rocks along the way, I would sing my favorite Primary songs. One of them seemed especially fitting for my walk home:

Sing your way home at the close of the day.
Sing your way home; drive the shadows away.
Smile ev'ry mile, for wherever you roam
It will brighten your road, it will lighten your load
If you sing your way home.

("Sing Your Way Home" [*Children's Songbook*, no. 193]).

Even now on occasion, after a busy day of teaching school, I find myself thinking of that song. I am grateful for the many other Primary songs I still treasure and keep close to my heart. It is like having a pocketful of encouragement that can be accessed anytime I need it. From these songs I learned that I am a child of God and that He has sent me here. I learned that my life has a plan and a purpose, and that my Father in Heaven wants me to be happy and choose the right. Primary songs taught me about a Baby who was born in a manger and grew up to save the world from sin. Primary songs showed me that Jesus loves me and that I should try to be like him. From Primary songs, I learned that the Lord needs me to shine for Him just as a sunbeam shines each day. I loved singing about the golden plates, and I know scriptures have power and can keep me safe from sin. I follow the prophet because he knows the way. I know that apricot blossoms can look like popcorn, and that snowmen will melt small, small, small. I have learned that if you're happy you should show it, and if you have a frown you can turn it upside down. I have learned it is wise to build a house on a rock and not on sand. I know that Nephi had courage. I try to do right, I try to be true, and I try to stand for the right in all that I do. I have learned about the temple and that families can be together forever through Heavenly Father's plan. I know He loves me and hears and answers every child's prayer.

Children, youth, and adults all over the world sing the songs of the gospel. Wherever we go, the messages of Primary songs can lift and comfort us throughout our lives. "And it shall come to pass that the righteous shall be gathered out from among all nations, and shall come to Zion, singing with songs of everlasting joy" (Doctrine and Covenants 45:71).

Wrapped in Peace

One day after skiing, my hands were so cold that I had a hard time unwrapping my fingers from the ski poles. Another day while ice skating, my hands and toes got so numb that when I ran cold water over them, the water felt hot. In my childhood, there were days when I couldn't stop shivering until my mom placed a warm quilt around me and told me to stand over the furnace vent to stop my teeth from chattering.

The dictionary defines "cold" as being without warmth, but another meaning is a feeling of being detached, discouraged, depressed, sad, or gloomy (see Dictionary.com). "Cold" can refer to being far away from something that is being sought. "Cold" can also refer to the sensation or feeling produced by a loss or absence.

All of us have had days when we felt discouraged, detached, depressed, or sad. There are many challenges in life that can leave us feeling cold—and I'm not talking about temperature here. We experience disappointments, broken hearts, health problems, unmet expectations, seemingly unanswered prayers, shattered dreams, and many other bumps in the road of life. Elder Robert D. Hales taught: "When the challenges of mortality come, and they come for all of us, it may seem hard to have faith and hard to believe. At these times, only faith in the Lord Jesus Christ and His Atonement can bring us peace, hope and understanding. Only faith that He suffered for our sakes will give us the strength to endure to the end" ("Finding Faith in the Lord Jesus Christ," Oct. 2004 General Conference).

Like me, when you are physically cold, you might reach for a warm quilt. And just as a quilt is made by connecting small pieces of fabric, so your faith in Jesus Christ is built by small, everyday experiences that are woven together. Your lifetime of faith will bring you the comfort promised by the Savior when He said: "Peace I leave with you, my peace I give unto you: not as the world giveth, give I unto you. Let not your heart be troubled, neither let it be afraid" (John 14:17).

When life seems cold, we can rely on the Lord Jesus Christ. We can trust in Him. As we do, the warmth will come.

Take Part

One Saturday morning, I got up early to start on my "To Do" list for the day. The garden needed to be weeded, the chicken coop and the house needed to be cleaned, and there were many other Saturday chores to do.

I dressed in old clothes, put on my work shoes, and found an old pair of gloves. Just when I was ready to head outside, the phone rang. It was the ward Primary president, asking if I could come to the stake baptism that day to lead the music, since the person they had planned on couldn't make it. I glanced at the clock and for a moment thought about all the other things I had to do that day. I would have to hurry, since the baptism was starting in fifteen minutes. I took a deep breath and said, "Sure." I quickly changed into a dress and hurried out the door.

As I walked into the Relief Society room a few minutes later, the families of the children being baptized were already seated. I wondered why someone else couldn't have filled in to lead the music. I took a deep breath, placed a hymn book on the music stand, and found a seat.

The bishop soon welcomed everyone and announced the program. I stood up to lead the opening song, still thinking about everything I had planned to do that day. The pianist started to play, and I raised my hand to start the song. I smiled at the two beautiful children sitting on the front row, waiting to be baptized. They were pure and clean and dressed in white, as were their fathers. Then the song began. "I am a child of God and He has sent me here." Those twelve words were all my voice would sing before the Spirit let me know, emphatically, that this was exactly where I needed to be on that Saturday morning. With tears streaming down my face, I smiled and kept leading the music as I seemed to hear the words "Susan, you are a child of God, and He has sent you here. He has given you and earthly home with parents kind and dear" (*Children's Songbook*, no. 2).

My heart was full that day and my spirit was lifted because I accepted a change in my agenda. Yes, someone else could have led the music at that stake baptism, but Heavenly Father knew I needed to participate. He knew I needed to hear the words of "I Am a Child of God" and be reminded that wherever I am, whatever I am doing on any given day, I am always His child and He is always aware of me.

That day I was lifted and blessed to be able to "Serve the Lord with gladness: (and) come before his presence with singing" (Psalm 100:2). Members of the Lord's true Church will always have opportunities to take part and serve. On those occasions, when your own "To Do" list gets full, remember that "one thing is needful" (Luke 10:42). When you do that, you will be able to "choose that good part" (ibid). As you put your faith into action by accepting the Lord's invitations to serve, you are the one being served.

Warm, Safe, and Happy

At bedtime when my children were small, I would tuck them into their beds, warm and safe for the night. On days when the wind blew and storms came, it felt wonderful to have everyone safe and sound under the same roof. Later in the evening, the last thing I would do before going to bed myself was to peek into the children's rooms to make sure all was well. Finally, I would turn off the porch light and lock the front door.

I remember helping my children get ready to play in the snow. It was quite the process to find boots that fit, gloves that matched, and hats, snow pants, and coats for everyone. When the kids were ready, they looked like an army of puffy little snowmen that had been dipped in a hodgepodge of colors.

I will never forget the first night after my oldest daughter moved away for her freshman year of college. Out of habit I walked by her room to peek in on her, only to remember she wasn't there. As I locked the front door and turned off the porch light, I wondered if my little girl, now all grown up, had everything she needed to be warm and safe and happy.

That night as I knelt by the side of my bed, I asked Heavenly Father to bless this daughter—to guide her through any storm or challenge that might come her way. I asked him to help her to continue to do the things that would strengthen her testimony. President David O. McKay taught: "There is nothing which a man can possess in this world, which will bring more comfort, more hope and faith than a testimony of the existence of a Heavenly Father who loves us, or the reality of Jesus Christ his only begotten Son" (*Teachings of Presidents of the Church: David O. McKay*, Chapter 17: "A Testimony of the Truth" [2003, 2011]).

The little gloves and boots are still in the box under the stairs, but the children who first wore them have grown up. Now I get to watch my grown children dressing their little ones in warm clothing so they can play in the snow. On occasion, I even get to watch my kids tuck their children into bed at night, teaching these precious souls and helping them gain the most important thing they can ever possess—a testimony of Jesus Christ.

A Constant Companion

All of us have gotten lost before, and it can be a very stressful experience. One night after speaking at a Young Women camp in Emigration Canyon, Utah, I got lost traveling home. Instead of going the long way through Logan, I thought I would take a shortcut my dad always used to take through Cache Junction. It was late at night, and I was alone without a GPS. After a few turns I wasn't sure about, I found myself on a muddy road in the middle of nowhere.

I finally stopped the car to try to figure out where I was. There were lights behind me, which must have been from Preston. To the left of me, closer to the mountain, were many lights from what I hoped was the big Pepperidge Farms plant. I said a brief prayer and decided to go back the way I had come and then head toward the lights. And I made it home.

It doesn't matter where you live or what your address is in this big world. Heavenly Father loves you and has prepared a way to help you return to Him. You have the precious gift of the Holy Ghost to light your path and guide you. You need not wander and become lost.

In April 2017 general conference, Elder Ronald A. Rasband declared: "My message today focuses on the importance of the Holy

Ghost in our lives. Our Father in Heaven knew that in mortality we would face challenges, tribulation, and turmoil; He knew we would wrestle with questions, disappointments, temptations, and weaknesses. To give us mortal strength and divine guidance, He provided the Holy Spirit, another name for the Holy Ghost" ("Let the Holy Spirit Guide").

The Holy Ghost is like a Gospel Positioning System you can use to orient yourself anytime during your life's journey. When you live worthily and ask for the Spirit to be with you, He will be your constant companion. The prophet Nephi said: "For behold, again I say unto you that if ye will enter in by the way, and receive the Holy Ghost, it will show unto you all things what ye should do" (2 Nephi 32:5).

That night when I got lost, I stopped to look for lights and reorient myself. This allowed me to get back on the right road and make it home. On those days when we become spiritually lost, we can look to the divine guidance of the Holy Ghost.

Listen Closer

On a hot Sunday in July with no air conditioning in our old meetinghouse, it was especially warm in Primary. As Primary president, I was concerned about the heat, especially since our Junior Primary room was located upstairs. I walked down the hall to check on the teachers and children in their classrooms, where all the doors and windows were open in hopes that even a slight breeze would come up. With each step I took and every open door I passed, sweet sounds—the gospel of Jesus Christ being taught to some of God's children—drifted into my heart. Scriptures were being read, songs were being sung, and small voices were answering questions about Jesus. My heart almost burst with love for these children and for the teachers who serve them.

Years later while serving in the stake Primary, I had a similar experience. One of the presidency's responsibilities was helping with the monthly stake baptisms. At a baptism one Saturday, my job was to guide the children from the hallway into the font, and to hand them a towel after they were baptized. I waited in the hallway, listening to the sounds of the gospel in action: the whispered instructions to a nervous father preparing to baptize his oldest daughter; the sound of water moving as father and daughter entered the font; the baptismal prayer and the *amen*; and finally the splash of water as a child was baptized a member of The Church of Jesus Christ of Latter-day Saints.

When my husband and I were called to serve together in the Brigham City Temple, I had the opportunity to see and hear the gospel in action inside the house of the Lord. Many times I walked down the hallway listening to reverent whispers as temple workers dressed in white welcomed and assisted the patrons. As I walked past sealing rooms, I heard the sweet sound of families being blessed with forever together. And at the veil of the temple, I listened to quiet voices that were like a hum of celestial music as a precious ordinance for departed loved ones was completed.

King Benjamin taught how important it is to hear the things of eternity: "You that can hear my words which I shall speak unto you this day; for I have not commanded you to come up hither to trifle with the words which I shall speak, but that you should hearken unto me, and open your ears that ye may hear, and your hearts that ye may understand, and your minds that the mysteries of God may be unfolded to your view" (Mosiah 2:9).

The next time you are at a baptism or in the temple, close your eyes for a minute and listen closely to the sweet sounds of the gospel in action. There simply isn't a better way to be lifted.

Kids These Days

My daughter Torie, who is an elementary school librarian, told of an experience she had with some students. While getting a class ready for an earthquake drill, she taught them that if an earthquake occurred while they were in the library, each student should quickly get under a table and cover his or her head. There were a few special-needs children in this class, including one young girl with severe disabilities who was dependent on others for just about everything. We will call her Sarah. She could not communicate, had little control over her arm movements, and often made loud noises. While Torie was giving instructions for the upcoming earthquake drill, one girl got up and walked over to sit closer to Sarah.

Soon the announcement came over the intercom to start the earthquake drill. Torie reminded the students of what they needed to do. The girl who had moved to sit by Sarah stood up and pulled Sarah up to stand beside her. Next, the girl patiently guided Sarah to a table and got under it, then gently pulled Sarah under the table to sit next to her. Instead of placing her hands on her own head for protection, the girl placed her hands over Sarah's head to protect her. Following this wonderful example, two other students put their hands over Sarah's head. Through their kindness, these students had created a holy place underneath a table in the library.

While my daughter Torie was on break duty in the playground that day, a young girl with crippled feet had a race with her two best friends. The three girls stood next to each other as if at a starting line and then took off running. With smiles, giggles, and a swinging ponytail, the little disabled girl ran as fast as she could. Her two best friends ran slowly so they wouldn't pass her, and at the finish line, she was pronounced the winner.

That same day, Torie witnessed a four-square game where all but one of the participants were fourth-grade boys. The lone third-grade boy struggled with communication and social interaction. The older children quickly reinvented the game to include their special new friend. When Joey would miss the ball, the other boys would help him. When he would kick the ball out, they would call it the Joey Ball. While cheering him on, they would help him move up to the king's square. With a big smile on his face, Joey would jump up and down and wait until he got the ball again. He was all smiles, simply because a handful of our Father in Heaven's children were sharing their light.

Just before the last bell rang that day, Torie saw a first-grade girl kneeling on the "Buddy Bench." The girl's arms were folded, her head was bowed, and her eyes were closed. Thinking the girl was crying, Torie walked over to check on her. The little girl opened her eyes, looked at Torie, and said with a smile, "I forgot to say my prayers this morning." Then the girl jumped down and skipped over to the monkey bars.

Sometimes people talk about "kids these days" in an unfavorable light. But when I see these latter-day angels in action, I am reminded whose these children really are, and the purpose of their being born in the latter days. In John we read, "While ye have light, believe in the light, that ye may be the children of light" (John 12:36). Every day my spirit is lifted as I watch these modern "children of light" bless the lives of others.

After he became President of the Church, Ezra Taft Benson said to a gathering of youth in Southern California: "For nearly six thousand years, God has held you in reserve to make your appearance in the final days before the Second Coming. . . . God has saved for the final inning some of his strongest children, who will help bear off the kingdom triumphantly. . . . Each day we personally make many decisions that show where our support will go. The final outcome is certain—the forces of righteousness will finally win. What remains to be seen is where each of us personally, now and in the future, will stand in this fight—and how tall we will stand" ("In His Steps," Church Educational System Fireside, 8 Feb. 1987).

I love "kids these days," and just like my daughter Torie, I have witnessed firsthand their shining examples of faith, love, and charity. They are some of the "strongest children saved for God's final inning" and I have no doubt that "they will bear off the kingdom triumphantly" (Benson, ibid). These young people are following the Savior's instructions found in the Book of Mormon: "Hold up your light that it may shine unto the world. Behold I am the light which ye shall hold up—that which ye have seen me do" (3 Nephi 18:24).

Keep an eye out for "kids these days." There are champions of light are all around you. Your heart will be lifted by their goodness and their example.

Holding onto Hope

A few nights ago, the sky was colored in beautiful cobalt blue with millions of stars. Awe and reverence filled my soul as I gazed at the sky and thought of He who created those stars. God Himself declared: "And worlds without number have I created; and I also created them for mine own purpose; and by the Son I created them, which is mine Only Begotten" (Moses 1:33).

Did you see the sunrise today? Every sunrise is a beacon of hope, for we know who created all light. "And God said, let there be light: and there was light. And God saw the light, that it was good: and God divided the light from the darkness" (Genesis 1:3–4).

Just as the sunrise shuts the gates of darkness and brings the light of a new day, hope closes the doors of doubt and brings light to the soul. Hope is the light that guides our feet. Hope looks to the future and its promised blessings. Hope is confidence waxed strong. Hope is courage that leads to faith and action. Hope is patient perseverance.

Elder Jeffrey R. Holland stated: "Every one of us has times when we need to know things will get better. Moroni spoke of it in the Book of Mormon as 'hope for a better world' (Ether 12:4).

For emotional health and spiritual stamina, everyone needs to be able to look forward to some respite, to something pleasant and renewing and hopeful, whether that blessing be near at hand or still some distance ahead. It is enough just to know we can get there, that however measured or far away, there is the promise of good things to come" ("An High Priest of Good Things to Come," Oct. 1999 General Conference).

Hold onto "the hope that is in you" (1 Peter 3:15), which is a gift from a loving Heavenly Father. Just as we know the sun will rise, we do not doubt the dawn. Such is the message of hope.

Plan on His Plan

As a schoolteacher, I am required to prepare lesson plans. A few years ago, my principal recommended a book on lesson planning. The book explains how to create lesson plans by focusing on an enduring, durable understanding of the things one desires to teach. The ideas in this book compelled me to center my planning on what was truly important—bottom-line kinds of things that my students would really need to know and understand to live productive lives.

Our Father in Heaven has prepared lesson plans to guide each of us and help us focus on what is enduring and durable in our own lives. Elder Yoshihiko Kikuchi said: "You were once in His holy presence. I know that your Heavenly Father has a special plan for you and your family to return to live with Him" ("Heavenly Father Has a Special Plan," Apr. 2000 General Conference).

I grew up in Bear River City with the best parents in the world. My two brothers liked to catch catfish and tease girls, and my little sister played house with me and was really good at getting out of doing the dishes. I loved my family and grew up loving the gospel of Jesus Christ. When I started in Young Women, I started making plans for my life—graduate from high school, go to college, get married in the temple, raise a family, teach school, retire early to go on a mission with my husband, and grow old together sitting on the front porch in our rocking chairs.

We all make plans, set goals, and prepare for the future. And these are good things to do. But sometimes what we have planned for our lives is not the lesson plan that our Father in Heaven has prepared. Because of His infinite love for us, His focus is on what we need to learn and understand in order to gain eternal life.

Five years ago, my life's plans changed. The day my husband was called to heaven, the words to a Primary song kept going through my mind: "My life is a gift, my life has a plan. My life has a purpose in Heaven it began" ("I Will Follow God's Plan for Me," *Children's Songbook,* no. 164). Unexpectedly losing Steve brought me great sorrow, and I couldn't help but wonder how my life would be. What lesson did God want me to learn? We know that Heavenly Father doesn't send us every trial or challenge, and that many of these come simply because we are mortal. We also know that death is an essential part of the plan of salvation. But I couldn't help wondering why a lifetime of gospel living hadn't been enough to allow my husband and me to grow old together.

It is disappointing when life doesn't turn out as we would like it to. There are days when I feel devastated about the loss of my husband. I don't have all the answers about what Heavenly Father wants me to do, and you probably feel the same way about your life. But I do know that all of our trials and challenges will help prepare us to live with Him again someday.

Plan your life, but remember that your Father in Heaven knows best and will—if you remain faithful—bless you according to His great plan of salvation.

The Promise of Joy

Life is not always easy. In fact, sometimes it is indescribably hard. How do we find happiness on days and months and maybe even years when life seems too difficult to bear? Elder Dallin H. Oaks explained: "Joy is more than happiness. Joy is the ultimate sensation of well-being. It comes from being complete and in harmony with our creator and his eternal laws" ("Joy and Mercy," Oct. 1991 General Conference).

Happiness is based on what happens, but joy can remain even amid suffering. Happiness is what we feel when things are going well; joy is what we feel because we know all will be well. Happiness comes and goes, but joy stays. Happiness is a present-state emotion. Joy is an emotion of expectation and anticipation of something great or wonderful. Happiness is fleeting, while joy is a gift that no one can take from you. Happiness can fill a moment; joy is a fruit of the Spirit that can fill your entire soul. Joy is something you can feel no matter what else is going on around you.

Elder Russell M. Nelson declared that "the joy we feel has little to do with the circumstances of our lives and everything to do with the focus of our lives. When the focus of our lives is on God's plan of salvation . . . and Jesus Christ and His gospel, we can feel joy regardless of what is happening—or not happening—in our lives. Joy comes from and because of Him. He is the source of all joy. . . . Joy is powerful, and focusing on joy brings God's power into our lives" ("Joy and Spiritual Survival," Oct. 2016 General Conference).

What a wonderful promise—that focusing on joy brings the power of God into our lives. We truly can feel joy in our present circumstances, whatever they are. Joy comes when we understand that there is more than today and more than this life. If our joy starts to dim, we only need to open our scriptures or listen to the words of our modern prophets for a reminder that God loves us. Because of that love, He wants His children (all of us!) to feel joy. It is part of the great plan of redemption, for as Lehi declared, "Adam fell, that men might be; and men are, that they might have joy" (2 Nephi 2:25).

"If we look to the world and follow its formulas for happiness," Elder Russell M. Nelson continued, "we will never know joy. The unrighteous may experience any number of emotions and sensations, but they will never experience joy! Joy is a gift for the faithful. It is the gift that comes from intentionally trying to live a righteous life, as taught by Jesus Christ" ("Joy and Spiritual Survival," ibid).

As you focus on "the joy that [is] set before [you]" (Hebrews 12:2) and "feel the Savior's Atonement working in your life" (Nelson, ibid), you can rise above the pessimism, disappointment, and gloom of the world. Your testimony of the gospel gives you an eternal perspective that allows you to see beyond your present cares. Let yourself feel joy in little everyday things—the laughter of a child, the kind smile of a stranger, the beauty of nature—and in the things of eternity. Be confident in the Lord's promise that in the next life, everything will be made right and there will be no more tears of sadness (see Revelation 21:4).

Pink Bears and Peanut Butter

As a member of a ward Relief Society presidency, I was blessed with many opportunities to help others, and in return to have my own heart lifted. One such chance began when I received a phone call from a worried grandmother who lived some distance away. She expressed concern about her daughter, a young mother who was home ill with her three young daughters. Her husband had been called into work, and the little girls were trying to take care of themselves and their mom.

I told the grandmother not to worry and that I would go right over to her daughter's house. Then I called Kay, our Relief Society president, and we went over together. We knocked on the young woman's door and heard little voices and the scurrying of little feet. Soon the door swung open. Three beautiful little girls stood there, dressed in pink and peanut butter. A trail of toys, bears, and dress-up clothes led us to the couch where the ill mother lay. It was clear that she was suffering from a high fever, but her eyes were full of her concern for her daughters. Nothing else needed to be said. Kay and I helped her into bed and assured her that we were there to help and to make sure she could rest and get well.

Kay and I cleaned the kitchen, put away the peanut butter, and got three little angels ready for bed. We sang a lullaby to the baby and tucked her safely into her crib for the night. Next, we walked down the hall and into the bedroom to put the other two little girls to bed. The room was painted in everything a little girl would love—pink bears, princess costumes, and dolls. We turned down the sheets on two little beds and told the girls it was time for bedtime prayers. Kay reminded each of them to ask Heavenly Father to bless their mommy to get better. Then we all knelt down together. Kay and I listened as two little angels took turns talking to their Heavenly Father about their parents and their baby sister, and even thanking Him for the people who had come to help.

Elder Jeffrey R. Holland testified of the magnificent days we will have if we will be faithful: "If we give our heart to God, if we love the Lord Jesus Christ, if we do the best we can to live the gospel, then tomorrow—and every other day—is ultimately going to be magnificent, even if we don't always recognize it as such. Why? Because our Heavenly Father wants it to be! He wants to bless us" ("Tomorrow the Lord Will Do Wonders among You," May 2016 General Conference).

How grateful I am to be a witness to yet another of Heavenly Father's masterpiece moments on a day of pink bears and peanut butter.

Worthy Goals

One year I wanted to encourage my students to not only set goals, but to persevere and accomplish those goals. I began with a story about a young boy who planned to be a dragon fighter when he grew up. Then each student made a shield and hung them on the back wall of our classroom. During the school year, each student would set a goal of something he or she wanted to be better at—spelling, math, reading, sleeping through the night without having to wake up Mom and Dad, and other things a third-grader might struggle with. When a student accomplished a goal, the student would get his or her shield, stand on a chair, and say out loud for everyone to hear, "I am a dragon fighter!"

At the end of the school year, I asked my students to write in their journals what they had learned about setting goals and what it means to be a dragon fighter in third grade. Here are some of the things they wrote:

- "Some people ask what it means to be a dragon fighter. It means you work hard to achieve something."

- "A dragon fighter is someone who fights obstacles, something you want to get better at."
- "A dragon fighter needs to be brave even if he feels fear."
- "When someone asks a dragon fighter where his or her armor is, you just say you don't have armor. Instead, you have power deep down inside of you. You have a sword called a pencil and you have a shield you use for mistakes called an eraser. That is your armor that you use to fight a dragon and reach a goal."
- "A dragon fighter means you are trying to beat something you are bad at, something you want to become better at."
- "A dragon fighter is a saying that means you can fight something that is hard for you. Sometimes I know I am not good at something, so I try. I try to accomplish it and to be better at it."
- "To be a dragon fighter means you complete your goal. You improve your skills."
- "People need to try. You always get better at something when you try."
- "Nobody is perfect, not even dragon fighters. So don't worry, just keep trying, and as a dragon fighter you will always be perfect at trying."

Elder Dallin H. Oaks spoke of the importance of setting goals: "Another source of happiness and mortal joy is the accomplishment of worthy goals, simple things like physical exercise or more complex goals like the completion of an arduous task. Other goals have eternal significance. Their completion produces joy in this life and the promise of eternal joy in the world to come" ("Joy and Mercy," Oct. 1991 General Conference).

Setting and accomplishing goals helps us become the kind of person we need to become—even a dragon fighter.

Who You Really Are

While my husband was serving as a stake high councilor, his turn came to speak in sacrament meeting at the Bear River Valley Senior Care Center. He asked me to speak with him. I was happy for the opportunity and felt blessed because at the time, my mother was a resident at the center.

Since there wasn't an assigned topic, I prayed about what I could say to these wonderful brothers and sisters who had served in the Church all of their lives. Early one morning, the thought came that I should simply remind them of who they are. So, when the time came for my talk, I started out with a Primary song, but I changed the pronouns. Here is the third verse of the song with those tweaks:

[You are] a child of God.
His promises are sure;
Celestial glory shall be [yours],
If [you] can but endure.

("I am a Child of God," *Children's Songbook*, no. 2)

That day at the senior center, as I looked into the faces in front of me, I could feel the love that Father in Heaven had for each of these sweet people. Regardless of your age, your situation in life, or where you reside, you are loved. You are God's child, and indeed "His promises are sure" (ibid).

Elder Richard G. Scott testified: "It is not sufficient to have a vague understanding of truth or the reality of the Father and His Son, our Savior. Each of us must come to know who They really are. You must feel how very much They love you. You must trust that as you consistently live the truth the best you can, They will help you realize the purpose of your earth life and strengthen you to qualify for the blessings promised" ("Truth Restored," Oct. 2005 General Conference).

One of the most important things you can learn and internalize is that you are a child of God. He knows you better than you know yourself. He knows what you can be. He sees you trying to obey Him. He sees your good works, and he sees the tribulations you go through. He is always reaching out to each of His children, and that includes you. Let yourself trust in His perfect love.

Purpose in Prayer

When I was a little girl, my mom helped me learn how to pray. With the blankets turned down and my stuffed pink hippopotamus waiting by my pillow, I would kneel at the side of the bed, clasp my hands, close my eyes, and repeat my mother's words as she taught me how to speak to Heavenly Father.

After a lifetime of living, my understanding of prayer has expanded. I have learned to heed promptings to pray, and to listen to the Spirit's guidance about what to pray for. I have come to rely on my Heavenly Father and to know that He is anxious to bless all of His children. I am so grateful for the opportunity to speak to Him, and for the assurance that He always listens and will answer my prayers in His own will and in His own time.

We are not only *allowed* to pray to the God of the universe, but He *commands* us to do so. Jesus Christ told the assembled Nephites to "watch and pray always" 3 Nephi 18:15. President James E. Faust explained what prayer is: "First, prayer is a humble acknowledgment that God is our Father and that the Lord Jesus Christ is our Savior and Redeemer. Second, it is a sincere confession of sin and transgression and a request for forgiveness. Third, it is recognition that we need help beyond our own ability. Fourth, it is an opportunity to express thanksgiving and gratitude to our Creator . . . . Fifth, it is a privilege to ask Deity for specific blessings" ("The Lifeline of Prayer, Apr. 2002 General Conference).

President Faust mentioned asking Heavenly Father for blessings. What kind of blessings are we to pray for? Let's look to the Book of Mormon for the answer: "Cry unto him when ye are in your fields, yea, over all your flocks. Cry unto him in your houses, yea, over all your household, both morning, mid-day, and evening. Yea, cry unto him against the power of your enemies. Yea, cry unto him against the devil, who is an enemy to all righteousness. Cry unto him over the crops of your fields, that ye may prosper in them. Cry over the flocks of your fields, that they may increase. But this is not all; ye must pour out your souls in your closets, and your secret places, and in your wilderness. Yea, and when you do not cry unto the Lord, let your hearts be full, drawn out in prayer unto him continually for your welfare, and also for the welfare of those who are around you" (Alma 7:11–12).

Isn't that a reassuring passage of scripture? We can pray about anything we would like to pray about. We can ask any questions we want to ask. We can confide in our Heavenly Father. We can trust in Him.

Talk to Him in prayer. He is always there, waiting for you.

Learning from Mistakes

One of my favorite books is *Mistakes that Worked: 40 Familiar Inventions & How They Came to Be,* by Charlotte Foltz Jones and John O'Brien. The book describes everyday inventions that started out as mistakes. The title could've been *People Who Made Their Mistakes Work.* Here are a few examples from the book: Sticky notes were created when a man made glue that turned out not to be permanent. Potato chips were invented when a chef got angry at a customer who had complained that his fried potatoes weren't thin enough; the chef made the potatoes paper-thin just to show him, but the customer ended up liking the new crisp-fried "potato chips."

One year, my fourth-grade students were working on Halloween drawings, complete with a haunted house and ghosts. A student came up to my desk to show me that she had made a mistake and had erased so hard that she had torn a hole right through the center of the picture. She was crying because she thought her whole picture was ruined, and she wanted to throw it away. I told her there might be something we could do with her picture, and soon we had an idea. I asked her to draw a small picture of a ghost and cut it out. Next

I handed her a strip of paper and told her to fold it like a fan. We applied glue to both sides of the fan and stuck the fan right over the hole in her picture, then glued on the ghost to make it look as if the ghost was floating over the haunted house. Other students liked the idea and started doing the same thing to their pictures. Thanks to the first student's mistake, she ended up creating a piece of artwork that was better than she could have imagined.

When we make a mistake, we might feel like giving up. We may even berate ourselves and start thinking that we are terrible and sinful. But mistakes and sins are not the same thing. Elder Dallin H. Oaks declared: "I would say that a wrong choice in the contest between what is good and what is bad is a sin, but a poor choice among things that are good, better, and best is merely a mistake. . . . We should seek to avoid mistakes, since some mistakes have very painful consequences. But we do not seek to avoid mistakes at all costs. Mistakes are inevitable in the process of growth in mortality. To avoid all possibility of error is to avoid all possibility of growth" ("Sins and Mistakes," BYU Devotional [Provo, UT], 16 Aug. 1994).

If you think a mistake has ruined a relationship or even your life, remember Elder Oaks's counsel. Mistakes are inevitable and they allow us to learn and grow. In fact, someday you might look back on past mistakes and realize how the Lord turned them into priceless learning experiences.

The Power of Music

As a young child, I often awoke in the morning to the sound of my dad singing. I would lie in my bed listening to his voice and feeling happy and grateful. One of his favorite songs was "Mockingbird Hill":

When the sun in the morning peeps over the hill
and kisses the roses round my windowsill.
Then my heart fills with gladness when I hear the trill
of the birds in the treetops on Mockingbird Hill.

(lyrics by Carl "Calle" Jularbo, lyrics © T.R.O. Inc., Lyrics.com)

I love music. My sweet grandmother taught me my first notes on her old piano. I love the way a melody can fill the soul with peace and hope. From the strains of "A sunbeam, a sunbeam" ("Jesus Wants Me for a Sunbeam," *Children's Songbook*, no. 60), to the Spirit testifying to me now that "I know that my redeemer lives" (see *Hymns*, no. 136), the songs of the gospel bear witness of the truth. Whenever my heart needs a lift, I can always find it in the music of the gospel.

Russell M. Nelson taught: "Worthy music is powerful. It has power to make us humble, prayerful, and grateful. Prophets through all generations have taught the importance of worthy music in our expressions of worship" ("Power and Protection Provided by Worthy Music," May 2008 General Conference).

Let the songs of the gospel bear you up. "For my soul delighteth in the song of the heart; yea, the song of the righteous is a prayer unto me, and it shall be answered with a blessing upon their heads" (Doctrine and Covenants 25:12).

Superheroes You Know

A few years ago, I attended an art conference for educators. I was excited to learn new ideas to teach to my students, and anxious to share those ideas with other art teachers throughout Utah. What I got that day was not ideas of what my students could draw or paint; instead, I received an assignment to look for the superheroes in my life—people who have gone through hard times and have come out on top. That day, I learned how powerful it can be to admire someone who has made it to where we want to go.

Consider the success of Albert Einstein, who didn't speak until he was four years old. His teachers thought he was lazy and would never make anything of himself. But he kept thinking and went on to develop the theory of relativity. Benjamin Franklin's parents could only afford to keep him in school until he was ten years old. He taught himself and went on to invent the lightning rod and bifocals. Vincent Van Gogh is considered one of the greatest artists of all time, yet he only sold one painting in his lifetime. Even though he made very little money with his art, he still painted over nine hundred works of art. (See www. huggpost.com/entry/successful-people-obstacles.)

How would you define a hero? Sometimes we think of a hero as someone who is physically strong and who saves people. But I think a real hero is someone who can triumph over trials and withstand the buffetings of Satan. A hero is someone who will sacrifice time and talents to serve people who are in need. Look at your own life and you will quickly recognize the heroes all around you.

Many people have blessed my life and become role models for me. My mother was one of those heroes. She contracted polio when she was twenty-six years old, with three children under the age of five, and a fourth child on the way. After spending a month in the hospital and two months in a wheelchair, my mother worked through painful therapy and persevered until she could finally walk again. Each day she had the courage to move forward even though her world had been turned upside down. She discovered joy in the upside. For the rest of her life, she wore a back brace, but I never heard her complain about it. Whenever she was sick or down, she would fight to keep going, and she was a wonderful mother to us children.

People who choose to shine through the storms deserve our admiration. H. David Burton taught that "carefully selected heroes can give us a pattern for our lives and serve as our role models. They can give us courage to walk the road of life righteously" ("Heroes," Apr. 1993 General Conference).

The individuals we admire can be a great resource for learning, growth, and motivation. If you want to get ahead, find out how others did so. And if someone has impacted your life for the better, let that person know. Look for the heroes in your life and see what you can learn from them.

Highly Favored of the Lord

For many years I have kept a journal. I enjoy going back and reading through the memories of good times and challenges, joys and difficulties. When my husband passed away, I felt as though my life had been shattered. One night, I reached for my journal and found one blank page left. I picked up a pen and stared at the empty page, thinking of all the things Steve and I had planned for our lives as we got older—watching our grandchildren grow up, retiring, serving a couple's mission, and seeing the world. With him gone, none of these dreams could be fulfilled. Then I looked at the empty page again, and instead of a bucket list of the things my husband and I wouldn't get to do, I started making a list of the things we *had* done—those blessed moments we got to spend together. I wrote and cried, smiled and remembered, and then wrote some more. When I was finished and closed the book, I felt much like Nephi when he said, "I, Nephi, having been born of goodly parents, therefore I was taught somewhat in all the learning of my father; and having seen many afflictions in the course of my days, nevertheless, having been highly favored of the Lord in all my days; yea, having had a great knowledge of the goodness and the mysteries of God, therefore I make a record of my proceedings in my days" (1 Nephi 1:1). Despite losing my husband, I *have* been highly favored of the Lord in all of my days.

Pull out your journal and write down all the wonderful things that have happened in your life. Be sure to include both the expected and unexpected blessings from Heavenly Father. President Henry B. Eyring taught us "to find ways to recognize and remember God's kindness" ("O Remember, Remember," Oct. 2007 General Conference). Jot down notes whenever you think of something you want to include in your journal. Maybe it is a memory that makes you smile, or a time when you didn't think you could make it through the day but then the Lord lifted you with a tender mercy. Regularly record these precious experiences within the pages of a journal so you can look back on them anytime you need encouragement.

Built upon a Rock

Geology is a science that deals with the history of the earth and its life, especially as recorded in rocks. For the final exam for my Geology 101 college class, I had to memorize the characteristics and classifications of rocks, and learn to identify different rocks that were set out around the room. Rocks are classified according to characteristics—permeability, texture, and particle size. These physical properties are determined by the processes that form the rocks.

In 2015, construction began on the Cedar City Utah Temple. Huge boulders were lifted out of the ground and broken into smaller pieces to be used for the building's foundation. When I was the Primary music leader, one of the junior Primary's favorite songs was about a rock:

The wise man built his house upon the rock,
And the rains came tumbling down.
The rains came down, and the floods came up,
And the house on the rock stood still.

("The Wise and the Foolish Man," *Children's Songbook*, no. 281)

Rocks represent strength and stability. They can be a mainstay, fortification, and a stronghold for defense. A rock's properties include steadiness, firmness, and immovability. What rocks are in your "gospel rock" collection? What are the rocks you are building your life on that you can use as a stronghold for defense?

One of the rocks I am building my life on is a more serious study of the scriptures. The *Come, Follow Me* program has blessed my life as I focus more on growing closer to Heavenly Father and Jesus Christ through scripture study. Elder Richard G. Scott explained: "Our Father in Heaven understood that for us to make desired progress during our mortal probation, we would need to face difficult challenges. Some of these would be almost overpowering. He provided tools to help us be successful in our mortal probation. One set of those tools is the scriptures" ("The Power of Scriptures," Oct. 2011 General Conference).

My life is lifted each day as I carefully study my scriptures. I often refer to the Topical Guide and the Bible Dictionary to gain more insight. In a special notebook, I write down passages and messages that apply to my life that day. In another book, I write down scripture verses that stand out. I call this small book "My Rock Collection." I keep the book open by my desk, and each day I turn to a new page to be lifted by one of the "scripture rocks" in my collection. What are your favorite verses of scripture? Consider writing them down and glancing at one of them every day. What you learn from the scriptures can increase your firmness, steadfastness, and stability.

When We Fall

When I was young, I wanted to learn how to ice skate. But instead of having a nice new pair of figure skates that fit, I had to wear an old pair of men's hockey skates that were three sizes too big, which meant I had to wear three pairs of socks. My dad helped me lace up the skates and said he would teach me to skate.

The sharp narrow blades and the fact that the skates didn't fit properly made it very challenging. Instead of sliding across the ice, I mostly worked on just trying to stand up. I tried to keep my weak ankles straight as my dad instructed, and I held onto him as we tried to make our way across the ice. Day after day, fall after fall, we would try again and again. Each night I would put the skates in the box by the stairs, hoping to skate a little better the next day. Gradually, my ankles got stronger and I fell less often.

For Christmas that year, my little sister and I got our first pairs of figure skates. I still remember opening my box. My skates were beautiful, white, and exactly my size, with a longer blade that could help me balance better. My sister and I immediately put on our coats and headed out to the frozen ditch across the street to give our new skates a try. We stood up on the ice and pushed off. Soon we were sliding, gliding, and twirling.

You probably remember the first time you tried to ice skate or ride a bike—and the first time you fell. Of course you got up and tried again. Competitive figure skater Randi Hill explained: "The reality that no one tells you when you want to be a figure skater is that you are actually signing up to become a professional faller. You see, when you start taking lessons, the first thing an instructor teaches you is how to fall" (https://alvcoaching.com/what-i-learning-from -falling/). Learning to ice skate is not easy. Falling on the ice hurts; it's like falling on concrete. But as we keep trying—as we persist—we develop determination and resilience.

When we are learning something new, we sometimes fall, either literally or figuratively. And because falling isn't fun, we might be hesitant to get up and try again. But falling is a teacher too. President Thomas S. Monson declared that "One of God's greatest gifts to us is the joy of trying again, for no failure ever need be final" ("The Will Within," Apr. 1987 General Conference).

When failure threatens to keep you down, consider what you have learned and how you can improve. If everything were easy, there would be no challenge and no growth. We are here on earth to learn how to become like our Heavenly Father.

What Is Your Magic?

Many times during my teaching career, the tables have been turned, and instead of teaching my students, I have been taught by them. One such occasion started out with a new classroom theme, "What Is Your Magic?" I wanted the students to know that each of them was unique, with special talents and abilities. We talked about what talents are and about the importance of figuring out what ours are so we can develop them. To make it easy to remember, we called these talents our "magic."

At the end of the year, I assigned the students to write a journal entry about what they thought their magic was. A few of the students asked to read their entries out loud. As they read them, I was in awe. These eight- and nine-year-old children understood the concepts of talents, persistence, and fortitude better than many adults do. I copied down a few of the students' thoughts, then printed out the page and hung it near my desk at school. This is what these students wrote:

Magic is not a spell you cast or abracadabra. It is something deep down inside you. Sometimes your magic does not flick on just when you need to see deeper. Sometimes you must search for your magic. Magic is learning about things. Magic is something you enjoy. Sometimes you must be tough to find your magic and to be tough you must persevere. To persevere you must have courage. Magic is when you find something you are good at and then you keep doing it and learning more about it. To make more magic, you try it, you practice it, and you do it every day. That is what magic is all about. That is the magic that makes you special, and that is the magic you can give to others.

Every time I read these students' words, I think about what I can contribute to the world as I share my own "magic"—my talents and gifts—with others.

In his book *Standing for Something*, President Gordon B. Hinckley stated: "It is not enough just to live, just to survive. It is incumbent on each of us to equip ourselves to do something worthwhile in society—to acquire more and more light, so that our personal light can help illuminate a darkened world. And this is made possible through learning, through educating ourselves, through progressing and growing in both mind and spirit" ([New York City: Times Books, 2000], 67).

What are you good at? Is there something you really enjoy or would like to learn? Make a point to develop and share your unique talents and gifts with your friends and family and the world, "that all may be profited thereby" (Doctrine and Covenants 46:12).

A Thankful Heart

I am thankful for the first rays of sunlight that begin each new day. I am thankful for the cool, crisp air of fall. I am thankful for life, laughter, and loved ones. I am thankful for quiet moments and peaceful places, and for the chaos of a busy room full of family and friends. I am thankful for songs to sing, and melodies heard only in the heart. I am thankful for the earth, the clouds, the rain, and the stars at night. I am thankful for the miracle of hearing a newborn baby's first cry, and the miracle of watching my children grow. I am thankful for Heavenly Father's plan of happiness. I am thankful for joy here and for joys laid up above.

Over and over again, the scriptures counsel us to have a thankful heart and to express gratitude for every blessing from God. Here are just a handful of examples:

- "Come before His presence with thanksgiving" (Psalm 95:2).
- "With thanksgiving let your requests be made known" (Philippians 4:6).
- "Enter into His gates with thanksgiving" (Psalm 100:4).

- "Doing all things with prayer and thanksgiving" (Doctrine and Covenants 46:7).
- "Sing unto the Lord with thanksgiving" (Psalm 147:7).
- "[A]nd that ye live in thanksgiving daily, for the many mercies and blessings which He doth bestow upon you" (Alma 34:38).

Having a thankful heart lifts our sights so that we recognize the many blessings God gives us every day. Elder Neal A. Maxwell declared: "Remembering and counting our many blessings can humble us by reminding us of all the reasons we have to be thankful to God—not just today's reasons, but those relating to all our yesterdays . . . How far should our memories be rolled back? As a beginning, certainly the rollback should cover the length of our personal lives. It requires energy and intellectual honesty to keep it before us" (*A Wonderful Flood of Light* [Salt Lake City: Deseret Book Co., 1990], 51).

When we focus on the things we are grateful for, even in our times of trial, we develop the humility that is critical to our eternal salvation. What are you most thankful for? Start writing down your blessings and you will be amazed at how many you have been given. "Verily, verily, I say unto you, ye are little children, and ye have not as yet understood how great blessings the Father hath in his own hands and prepared for you" (Doctrine and Covenants 78:17).

Sweet Whisperings

When students are busily working in my art classroom, I often let them talk quietly—if the project doesn't require a lot of concentration. The noise level always seems to grow louder and louder until I have to remind the students to lower their voices. But there is something more effective than my reminders, and that is when one student starts to whisper. For whatever reason, at the sound of a whisper, the whole room suddenly goes quiet. This has made me realize that oftentimes the loudest thing one can hear is a whisper.

We live in a busy world of noise and clamor, and sometimes the noise level grows louder and louder. That's when we need to focus most on and listening to the whisperings of the Holy Ghost. Helaman wrote, "It was not a voice of thunder, neither was it a voice of a great tumultuous noise, but behold, it was a still voice of perfect mildness, as if it had been a whisper, and it did pierce even to the very soul" (Helaman 5:30).

I am so grateful for the whisperings of the Spirit of God. I remember feeling the Spirit come over me as a little girl in Primary when I bore my testimony for the first time. I remember the whisper of the Spirit when a

Young Women teacher testified of the importance of temple marriage. I remember the whisperings of the Spirit as I woke up on the morning of my own temple wedding, and my temple dress hanging there on the curtain rod in my room. I remember holding my baby girl for the first time and looking into her eyes as the Spirit whispered that she was indeed a daughter of God, just like me.

On countless occasions, the Holy Ghost has whispered to me of the glory and miracle of life. The orange sunset, the wild flowers at the edge of a mountain lake, sleeping babies snuggled in blankets, little shoes by the back door, and watching a daughter hold her own baby. "Yea, thus saith the still small voice, which whispereth through and pierceth all things, and often times it maketh my bones to quake while it maketh manifest" (Doctrine and Covenants 85:6).

Our Father in Heaven invites you to listen to the whisperings of His Spirit. His gentle voice will bring peace to your soul. Remember what He has whispered to you in the past, and be ready to hear His voice today and every day for the rest of your life. Listen, for God truly is speaking to you.

Confidence to Go Forth

Heavenly Father has created worlds without number, including the earth on which we live. He created His children and endowed us with divine gifts and powers. A knowledge that God is our Father gives us the confidence to "arise and go forth" (Doctrine and Covenants 133:10) and do everything He asks us to do.

While Joseph Smith and several companions were imprisoned in Liberty Jail, he received several revelations, including Doctrine and Covenants 121. Verse 45 of this section reads: "[T]hen shall thy confidence wax strong in the presence of God." We will feel confident in the presence of God if we have kept His commandments and "exercise[d] unwavering faith regardless of our circumstances" (see Michael John U. Teh, "Confidence in the Presence of God," Messages from the Doctrine and Covenants, churchofjesuschrist.org).

After my husband passed away, I kept wondering, "How can I live my life without him?" I knew Heavenly Father would always love me and watch over me, yet my confidence in myself wavered. So, I turned to the scriptures and studied the concept of confidence. Here are just a few of the verses I discovered:

- Hebrews 10:35–36: "Cast not away therefore your confidence, which hath great recompence of reward. For ye have need of patience, that, after ye have done the will of God, ye might receive the promise."
- Proverbs 3:25–26: "Be not afraid of sudden fear . . . For the Lord shall be thy confidence."
- Hebrews 3:14: "For we are made partakers of Christ, if we hold the beginning of our confidence steadfast unto the end."

Elder Matthew Carpenter said, "During mortality we are tested to see if we will choose good over evil. For those who keep His commandments, they will live with Him 'in a state of never-ending happiness' (Mosiah 2:41). To help us in our progression to become like Him, Heavenly Father has given all power and knowledge to His Son, Jesus Christ. There is no physical, emotional, or spiritual ailment that Christ cannot heal . . . Please remember that Jesus Christ is mighty in *how*" ("Wilt Thou Be Made Whole?" Oct. 2018 General Conference).

On those days when your confidence wanes, remember that the Lord is mighty in *how*. As you look to Him in every thought, "He'll strengthen thee, help thee, and cause thee to stand. Upheld by His righteous omnipotent hand" ("How Firm a Foundation, *Hymns*, no. 85).

Happy Like Jesus

In a bookstore, one particular book seemed to jump off the shelf at me. I picked up the book and looked at the cover, which featured a photograph from a reenactment of the baptism of Jesus Christ. What stood out most were the happy smiles on the faces of the actors portraying John the Baptist and Jesus. I thought about how happy the hosts of heaven must have felt when the Savior of the world was baptized.

By His example, the Savior taught us everything we need to do to be happy. We know He is a happy Person because living His gospel makes *us* happy.

One of my favorite heroes from the Book of Mormon is Ammon. In Alma 27:17–18, we read: "Now the joy of Ammon was so great even that he was full; yea, he was swallowed up in the joy of his God, even to the exhausting of his strength; and he fell again to the earth. Now was not this exceeding joy? Behold, this is joy which none receiveth save it be the truly penitent and humble seeker of happiness." In this passage, we read of Ammon's joy upon seeing the prophet Alma after many years of being apart. We also learn that Ammon was "truly penitent" and a "humble seeker of happiness."

From these verses and from other scriptural passages, we learn that happiness is not something that just comes to you with no effort on your part. Being happy is something you *do*—something you seek after. How do we do this? One way is to remind ourselves of the reason we have to rejoice. And what is that reason? Ammon gave the answer: "Yea, I say unto you, there never were men that had so great reason to rejoice as we, since the world began; yea, and my joy is carried away, even unto boasting in my God; for he has all power, all wisdom, and all understanding; he comprehendeth all things, and he is a merciful Being, even unto salvation, to those who will repent and believe on his name" (Alma 26:35).

Why was Ammon happy? Because of the gospel of Jesus Christ. Ammon lived the gospel and he shared it with others. I testify that we will be happy as we do those same things.

Share Your Light

One year as I prepared to teach a Relief Society lesson on gospel light, I asked my son Tanner for a refresher course about electricity. He explained that electricity is created by a flow of electrons around a circuit. The electrons travel along wires that connect the power source to the device (such as a lamp or other light) and back again. Some circuits have a switch. Turned off the switch creates a gap in the circuit, stopping the movement of electrons. Turning on the switch closes the gap and allows the electrons to flow, which makes the light bulb glow.

The light of the gospel can be compared to a circuit. When we obey the commandments and seek to follow the Lord, the circuit is complete. As we read in modern revelation, "That which is of God is light; and he that receiveth light, and continueth in God, receiveth more light" (Doctrine and Covenants 50:24). This means that as we receive and obey God's truth, we will receive more of His truth—more of His light.

Think about the effects of electricity in your life. One of these is that you can read or work in your house after it is dark outside. When the power is on or the battery is charged or the generator is working, then you can have light. Light can also help you see what lies ahead.

To charge our spiritual batteries, we do things like studying the scriptures, going to our church meetings, praying sincerely and regularly, serving others, fulfilling our callings, and spending time in the temple. When our spiritual light is charged, we are able to follow the Savior's admonition to the Nephites: "Therefore, hold up your light that it may shine unto the world. Behold I am the light which ye shall hold up—that which ye have seen me do" (3 Nephi 18:24).

In my ward, a young boy who sat on the front row in Primary always seemed anxious and agitated. Each week, a young girl would quietly move up to sit in the empty chair next to him. When the boy became agitated or anxious, she would put her arm around him or hold his hand. Even though his behavior never improved, this angelic girl continued to share her friendship with him. The light of her spirit and her service seemed to brighten the whole room. She was indeed one of "the children of light" (1 Thessalonians 5:5).

Because you are a literal child of God, you have been blessed with the power to shine—to share your light with the world. The prophet Isaiah declared, "And if thou draw out thy soul to the hungry and satisfy the afflicted soul; then shall thy light rise in obscurity, and thy darkness be as the noonday" (Isaiah 58:10). When you share your light—your testimony—with others, that light will continue to shine brighter and brighter "until the perfect day" (Doctrine and Covenants 50:24). That perfect day will be the Second Coming of the Lord Jesus Christ.

A Point of View

This year at school, my third-graders are learning to recognize different points of view as seen through the eyes of characters in a book. Although all the characters may face similar situations, each can have a very different perspective. One character may view a situation with worry and concern, another may see the situation as an opportunity to learn and grow, and still another may view the situation with lightheartedness and ease.

Each person has a unique point of view on life's experiences. My father was an artist, so I learned at a young age to see landscapes from an artist's perspective. For example, rust changes the color of barbed wire wrapped around an old fence post, and rust takes its toll on farm equipment. An artist sees the rust and uses the uniqueness of the texture to show the history of the old metal. A rainstorm won't let up, and water soon floods a concrete cellar, but the farmer feels the rain on his face and lifts his head in gratitude as his growing wheat receives needed moisture. A fire burns through the entangled foliage of a ripe old forest. The charred remains enrich the soil and bring new growth.

No matter how tough a situation seems, we can choose how we view it—how we feel about the situation. This gives us control over our emotions, instead of letting our emotions control us.

On an airline flight to visit my son, I chatted with the sweet elderly woman sitting next to me. She told me about a family who moved to a faraway city. A new neighbor asked how the family had liked their previous neighborhood. The response was that they hadn't liked it at all. Dogs were always barking, people were too nosey, and the weather was bad. The new neighbor told them, "Well, that is what you will find here." Another family who had moved in was asked the same question by the new neighbor: "How did you like your previous neighborhood?" The family answered, "We loved everything about it. The neighbors were friendly, the weather was beautiful, and it is a place we will always cherish." The new neighbor said, "Well, that is what you will find here."

There are things in our lives that we can't change. But instead of dwelling on them, we can lift our gaze and see the blessings we *do* have. One way to do this is to make a list of the things in your life that bring you joy. You can write your list in a journal or a notebook. You might write down how someone spoke kindly to you, or how the smile of a friend brightened your day. You might write about inspiration you have received from the Spirit, or special moments with your family.

Elder Rafael E. Pion taught, "The eternal perspective of the gospel leads us to understand the place that we occupy in God's plan, to accept difficulties and progress through them, to make decisions, and to center our lives on our divine potential" ("The Eternal Perspective of the Gospel," Apr. 2015 General Conference).

Thanks to the gospel of Jesus Christ, we can look at life with an eternal point of view. The Lord assures us that our "afflictions shall be but a small moment" (Doctrine and Covenants 121:7) and that if we endure to the end, we will receive eternal glory (see 2 Timothy 2:10, 1 Peter 5:10, 2 Corinthians 4:17, and Isaiah 35:10).

Talk about the Sometimes

Sometimes people bear testimony about immediate answers to prayer, such as the healing of a loved one, or the miraculous avoidance of an accident. These are beautiful examples of the blessings Heavenly Father bestows upon His children. Yet when we only testify of immediate answers to prayer, we are not giving the full story.

In general conference, Elder Brook P. Hales told of a woman named Pat who was completely blind by age eleven. As an adult, she graduated from college, got a master's degree, and became a speech language pathologist. Now I will quote Elder Hales: "Several years ago, Pat traveled to California to visit family members who were living there. While she was outside with her three-year-old nephew, he said to her, 'Aunt Pat, why don't you just ask Heavenly Father to give you new eyes? Because if you ask Heavenly Father, He will give you whatever you want. You just have to ask Him.' Pat . . . responded, 'Well, sometimes Heavenly Father doesn't work like that. Sometimes He needs you to learn something, and so He doesn't give you everything you want. . . . Heavenly Father and the Savior know best what is good for us and what we need'" ("Answers to Prayer," Apr. 2019 General Conference).

When we have offered heartfelt prayers, received priesthood blessings, and pled for a miracle, we can become disheartened when we don't receive our heart's desire or even an answer. Elder Hales continued: "Because of that perfect love [of Heavenly Father], He blesses us not only according to our desires and needs but also according to His infinite wisdom . . . The Father is aware of us, knows our needs, and will help us perfectly. Sometimes that help is given in the very moment or at least soon after we ask for divine help. Sometimes our most earnest and worthy desires are not answered in the way we hope, but we find that God has greater blessings in store" (ibid).

When a prayer isn't answered right away, we might wonder if Heavenly Father is hearing our petitions. But if every good deed was followed immediately by a blessing, and if every prayer was instantly answered in the affirmative, there would be no need for faith. This earth life wouldn't be a trial, and the entire plan of salvation would be thwarted. So when it feels as if the curtains of Heaven are shut, don't give up. Remember that God knows what will be best for you in the long run, from His perfect eternal perspective. Live correct principles. Keep praying in faith and humility, pouring out the desires of your heart. Then continue forward in patience. When the answer to your prayer does come, thank Heavenly Father and rejoice in His mercy. He will never forget you, and if you continue in faith, all of the righteous blessings you seek will come to you, whether in this life or the next.

Focused on Christ

One afternoon, my daughter and I were shopping at the mall and stopped for lunch at the food court. We got our food and found a place to sit. As we ate, we noticed the people around us—busy mothers with hungry children, teenagers focused on their phones, and frustrated people waiting in long lines to place their orders. There didn't seem to be very many smiling faces. My daughter and I were getting ready to leave when a young father came by, pulling a small wagon. Inside was a little boy who was grinning at a red balloon tied to the wagon. Perhaps Winnie the Pooh said it best: "No one can be uncheered with a balloon" (*The House at Pooh Corner*, A. A. Milne [Boston, MA: Dutton Books, 2018). In all the noise and confusion in the food court, one red balloon not only cheered that little boy, but cheered my daughter and me as we looked at each other and smiled.

We live in a world that is not always smiling and happy. We all experience challenges and sadness. But we can be happy much of the time despite the things that happen to us. The Lord Himself declared: "Wherefore, be of good cheer, and do not fear, for I the Lord am with you, and will stand by you; and ye shall bear record of me, even Jesus

Christ, that I am the Son of the living God, that I was, that I am, and that I am to come" (Doctrine and Covenants 68:6).

What a simple yet profound concept, that we find happiness by focusing on the Savior. He has promised to always be with us and to stand by us—if we will look to Him and follow Him.

President Ezra Taft Benson taught, "The Lord asked the question of His disciples, 'What manner of men ought ye to be?' He then answered His own question by saying, 'Even as I am.' (3 Ne. 27:27.) To become as He is, we must have Him on our minds—constantly in our thoughts. Every time we partake of the sacrament, we commit to "always remember him" (Moro. 4:3; Moro. 5:2; D&C 20:77, 79). (First Presidency Message: "Think on Christ," *Ensign*, Mar. 1989).

Becoming like the Savior is a daunting task, but as we try to constantly keep Him in our thoughts, we will have the desire to follow His example. Being kind to others and watching for opportunities to bless their lives is one thing we can do every day to become more like Him.

When your life is clouded over with busyness and commotion, take a moment to focus on Jesus Christ. Look to Him in all your comings and goings. Look to Him when you don't know which way to turn and you need a friend. Look to Him in times of joy. As you focus on Him, your soul will be lifted.

Stop, Drop, and Grow

One day at the beginning of a school year, I reminded my seventh-grade class what they should do if we ever had a fire at the school. These students had practiced many fire drills through the years. A few weeks later, the fire alarm rang. I told my students to leave everything on their desks and exit the building. As we entered the hallway, there was a faint smell of smoke. One student looked at me with a worried expression and said, "Mrs. Chadaz, is this a fire drill or a real fire?" I told him I wasn't sure but that even if the fire was real, he would know what to do because we had practiced so many times.

After we made it safely outside, I learned there had been a little smoke in the faculty room as a result of some burned popcorn in the microwave. When we got back to our classroom, I asked my students, "What would you have done if the fire had been real?" A boy raised his hand and responded, "If there was a real fire, I would run as fast as I could to get outside!" I was amazed that even my big seventh-graders still didn't understand why we have fire drills. So on the day of that particular fire drill, I explained again that in a school of twelve hundred students, it would be dangerous if everyone ran. The reason we practice for the "what ifs" is because in the event of an actual emergency, not knowing what to do could cause the greater tragedy.

In each of our lives, emergencies may come in the form of relationship problems, financial hardships, health issues, or a myriad of other trials. These hardships can bring feelings of insecurity, self-doubt, and uncertainty. Elder Neil L. Andersen taught: "By definition, trials will be trying. There may be anguish, confusion, sleepless nights, and pillows wet with tears. But our trials need not be spiritually fatal. They need not take us from our covenants or from the household of God" ("Trial of Your Faith," Oct. 2012 General Conference).

Trials and disappointments come to all of us. What is your plan for when these problems arrive? An emergency drill we learn in school is to stop, drop, and roll if your clothes catch on fire. When a fiery trial comes your way, try this drill: stop, drop, and grow. Stop and remember that Heavenly Father is always near. Drop to your knees and speak to Him. Then listen for the still small voice of the Holy Ghost and follow His counsel. Each time you do this, you will grow in strength and wisdom.

Hold Tight, Hang On

Years ago, our family went to Salt Lake City and toured the newly finished Conference Center. Near the end of the tour, we noticed a painting by Arnold Friberg titled *Mormon Bids Farewell to a Once Great Nation*. The painting depicts Moroni tenderly raising up his wounded father, Mormon, during the Nephites' final battle with the Lamanites.

As my family and I and the rest of our tour group stood studying this beautiful piece of artwork, I noticed there was just one leaf hanging from a tree branch at the top of the painting. I said out loud, "I wonder what Arnold Friberg wanted to say by including that last leaf." A member of our tour group said she thought he painted it to represent that the battle was over, and that the Nephite nation was coming to an end. We were all quiet as we considered this idea, and then my mom declared, "I disagree. I think the last leaf is hanging on." She explained that to her, the leaf meant that even amidst the destruction of war, there is still hope. When everything around Mormon and Moroni seemed to be falling, one leaf still held on.

I have never looked at the painting again without thinking of my sweet, optimistic, and courageous mother. In the Book of Alma we read,

"While many thousands of others truly mourn for the loss of their kindred, yet they rejoice and exult in the hope, and even know, according to the promises of the Lord, that they are raised to dwell at the right hand of God, in a state of never-ending happiness" (Alma 28:12).

Sometimes we may feel devastated by what is happening to us or happening in the world around us. At those times, we need to hold on to what we know is true and continue in the pattern of gospel living we have established. For example, when I get up in the morning, I look out at the sunrise, or go outside to watch it if I can. Then I get ready for the day. Next I say a prayer, even when I don't know what to say. My scriptures lay open on the table, reminding me to take time to be nourished by them. On Sunday mornings, I get ready and go to church. When I must go alone, I still go, and I smile, listen, learn, talk to others, and worship.

When times are tough, keep going in the pattern of gospel living that has become the foundation for your life. Hold fast to your faith in Jesus Christ. Hold on to the righteous principles that have brought you peace in the past. In short, hang on and hold tight. The Lord's grace is sufficient and His promises are sure.

About the Author

Susan Ramsdell Chadaz grew up in Bear River City, Utah. Her artist father taught her to paint, and she learned valuable life lessons from her sweet mother. Susan graduated from Utah State University, where she met her husband, Steve, at a dance. She earned a bachelor's degree in education with an emphasis in art and has worked as a schoolteacher for twenty-five years. Susan has four wonderful children and fourteen grandchildren. She speaks at math conferences around the country and has taught at BYU-I Education Week for the past five years. Susan loves to read, draw, paint, travel, play the piano, and spend time with her family. Her artwork, referred to as "Rusty Apple Art," is sold at festivals throughout Utah, Idaho, and Arizona. Susan's first published book was *So Blessed: Living in Gratitude Every Day* (2018). She also illustrated *The Book of Real Beauty for LDS Girls* (2017), a collaborative effort with her daughter, author Tarrah Montgomery. Susan enjoys hearing from readers and may be contacted at schadaz@gmail.com.

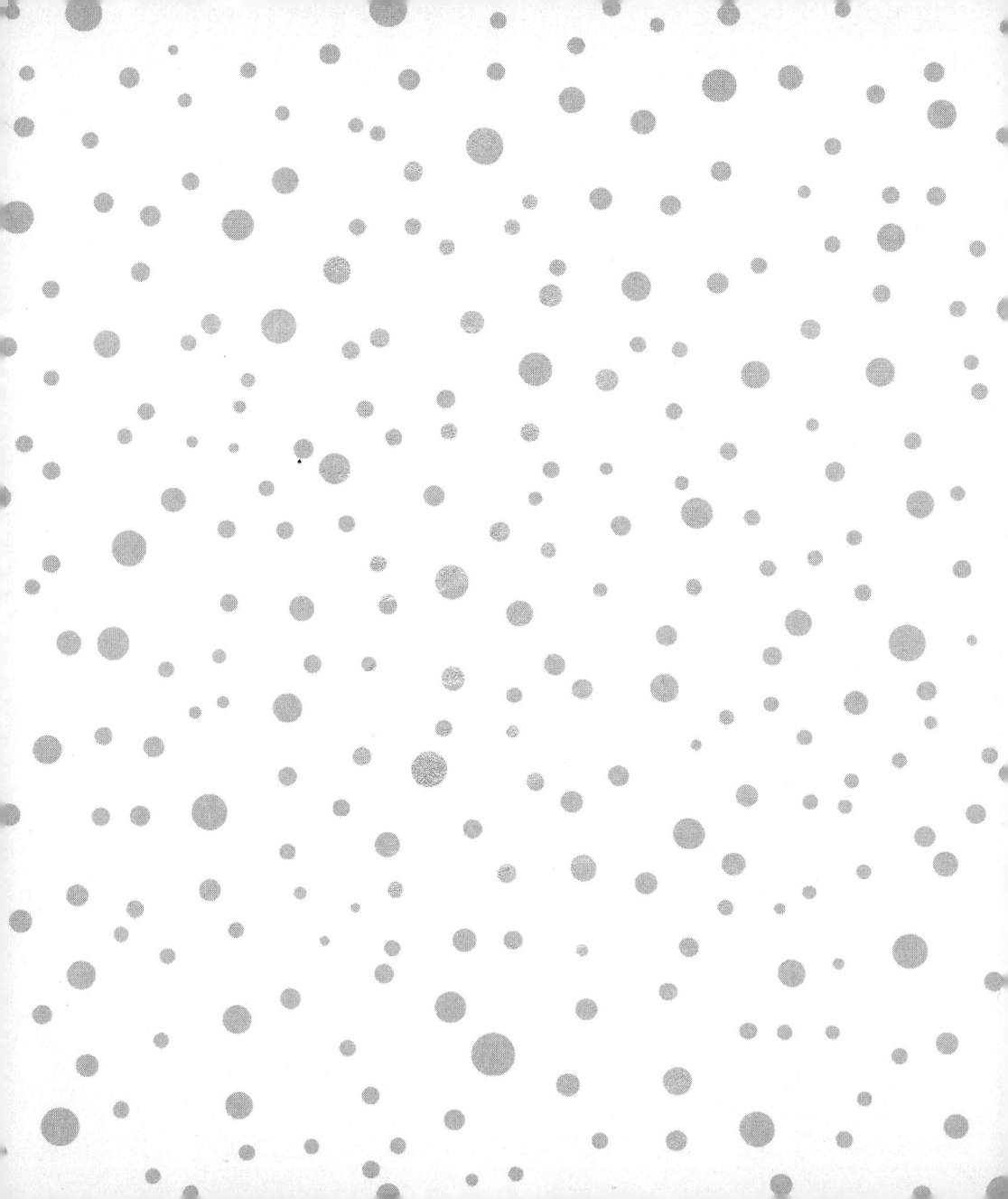